God Broke His Promise . . .

?

". . . and ye shall know my breach of promise."
Numbers 14:34

Art Barnes, Dr. of Ministry

with

Val Jean Barnes

© 1998 by Arthur A. Barnes

Published by Rainbow's End Company
354 Golden Grove Road
Baden, PA 15005

Art & Val Barnes
http://rainbows-end-publish.com
17569 Hwy. 14 N
Yellville, AR 72687

Publisher's Cataloging-in-Publication
(Provided by Quality Books, Inc.)

Barnes, Arthur A.
    God broke his promise? : traditional beliefs challenged by Scriptural truths / by Arthur A. Barnes. -- 1st ed.
    p. cm.
    Preassigned LCCN: 97-76658
    ISBN: 1-880451-26-3

    1. God--Promises. 2. God--Promises--Biblical teaching.
3. Jesus Christ--Person and offices. 4. Judaism (Christian theology) 5. Millennialism.   I. Title.

BT180.P7B37 1998   236.9
                            QBI97-41588

Dedication

I wish to dedicate this book to:

Reverend Raymond Vineyard, a Baptist minister, who was the first minister to encourage me in my ministry ...

Reverend Kirkendall who encouraged me in the Holy Spirit ...

The Bible School of Theology, San Jacinto, California ...

My companion in Christ, Val Jean Barnes who stands by me in spiritual love and understanding ...

And to all of those who have influenced me in my Christian walk.

Contents

PREFACE

Romans 10:1—Brethren, my heart's desire and prayer to God for Israel is that they might be saved.

Paul was burdened with the salvation of Israel. *If all of Israel would be saved, with or without Jesus, then why was Paul so concerned?* Because Israel, on the whole, had rejected and denied Christ, and, in so doing, had pronounced their own judgment on the day of Calvary.

Matthew 27:25—Then answered all the people, (Jews) and said, His blood be on us, and on our children.

What seems to be an innocuous theory has already condemned some souls to a misguided fate, while others will unnecessarily go through the tribulation.

The teaching that all Jews will be resurrected, living for 1000 years in the Millennium, and be given this time to make up their minds whether or not to accept Christ is, of course, a false doctrine from the enemy. When we examine the evidence, we can clearly see that such a belief is contrary to what

9

is taught in the Bible and contradicts the fact that Jesus Christ is the promised Messiah. It boggles my mind that some would believe this theory.

Israel is still trying to claim Palestine. Even if they manage to claim this small token, they will still fall far short of the vast area that God promised to Abraham. Also, Israel still does not have possession of the Holy Ground, the Temple does not exist, and the Ark has been lost.

INTRODUCTION

GOD'S PROMISES

Merrill Ungers Bible Dictionary gives four classes of promises in the Bible. They are:

1. Relating to the Messiah.
2. Relating to the church.
3. Relating to the Gentiles.
4. Relating to Israel.

Many Bible commentators who have written numerous books, pamphlets and tracts about the unconditional, irrevocable promises of God have failed to recognize the truth that these promises have been lost in antiquity.

Often, God's promises are found in conjunction with a covenant condition or requirement. A covenant promise is a promise made by God that contains a condition that must be honored by the one who receives it.

Because of disobedience, Abram never received his land promise. Likewise, Isaac never inherited the Promised Land.

Jacob sojourned in Egypt and never claimed the Promised Land of Canaan. And, because of their disobedience, the children of Israel lost their covenant promise and were dispersed to the four corners of the world.

The Abrahamic land promise will culminate at the end of time, during the Millennial Reign, and will include only those Jews who believe in Jesus as their Messiah. More on this later.

In the following chapters, we will deal with specific promises made by God, namely:

1. The promise to the seed.
2. The promise to the chosen.
3. The promise to the elect.
4. The promise to the remnant.
5. The promise to the brethren.
6. The promise to the heirs.
7. The land promise to Israel.
8. The promises to Abraham.
9. The promise to David.
10. The promise to Solomon.
11. The promise of a new name.
12. The promise of the regathering.
13. God's eternal promise.

CHAPTER ONE

THE PROMISE TO THE SEED

Genesis 12:7—And the Lord appeared unto Abram, and said, Unto thy seed will I give this land: and there builded he an altar unto the Lord, who appeared unto him.

Matthew 13:38—The field is the world; the good seed are the children of the kingdom; but the tares are the children of the wicked *one*.

I Corinthians 15:50-52—Now this I say, brethren, that flesh and blood cannot inherit the Kingdom of God; neither doth corruption inherit incorruption. Behold, I shew you a mystery; We shall not all sleep, but we shall all be changed. In a moment, in the twinkling of an eye, at the last trump: for the trumpet shall sound, and the dead shall be raised incorruptible, and we shall be changed.

Flesh and blood cannot inherit the Kingdom of God; neither does corruption inherit the Kingdom of God; neither does corruption inherit incorruption.

I ask, will a Jew, an Israelite who may be corrupt, who may be a thief, liar, murderer, or rapist, make Heaven his or her home only because he is of the seed of Abraham?

Will God, at the last trump, raise up Sodom and Gomorrah and give the inhabitants of those cities one thousand years to live in the Millennial, and finally, to make Eternal Heaven their home only because they are Abraham's seed? This is the contorted and twisted Gospel that some are teaching! *How wrong can man be?*

Ungers Bible Dictionary states that Hades or Sheol, the grave, is a place to ask or seek:

> **Luke 16:19-24**—There was a certain rich man, which was clothed in purple and fine linen, and fared sumptuously every day: And there was a certain beggar named Lazarus, which was laid at his gate, full of sores, And desiring to be fed with the crumbs which fell from the rich man's table: moreover the dogs came and licked his sores. And it came to pass, that the beggar died, and was carried by the angels into Abraham's bosom: the rich man also died, and was buried; And in Hell he lift up his eyes, being in torments, and seeth Abraham afar off, and Lazarus in his bosom. And he cried and said, Father Abraham, have mercy on me, and send Lazarus, that he may dip the tip of his finger in water, and cool my tongue; for I am tormented in this flame.

The rich man was buried in the grave and cried to Father

Abraham, asking for a drop of water to cool the tip of his tongue because he was in torment in the flames. I ask, will the rich man, being a Jew, make Heaven his home? Not according to:

> **Revelation 20:14-15**—And death and Hell were cast into the lake of fire. This is the second death. And whosoever was not found written in the Book of Life was cast into the lake of fire.

The rich man was Abraham's seed and, according to Matthew 13:38, God's promise was only to the Good Seed. God is no respecter of person, either Jew or Gentile. If the rich man's name is not found in the Lamb's Book of Life, he will be cast into the lake of fire on the final judgment day, to remain forever:

> **Revelation 20:10**—And the Devil that deceived them was cast into the lake of fire and brimstone, where the beast and the false prophet *are*, and shall be tormented day and night for ever and ever.

At one of the churches where I pastored, three members of the congregation were attending Bible college in preparation for the ministry. They informed me that the college was teaching that all Jews would be saved because Jesus, after He died on the Cross, descended into Hell and preached to the prisoners. In doing so, according to the college professors, He gave the Jews another chance to be saved.

With this in mind, I opened my Bible and shared the words of Luke 16:19-24 with the three students. Then, rhetorically speaking so they would know I was not speaking the truth, I turned to them and said in a mocking tone, "But

Abraham said, 'Son, wait just a little longer—Jesus will be coming down to Hell for a visit and to let you know that you'll have a thousand years to decide if you want to be saved!' " Sometimes the foolishness of speaking in this way is necessary to illustrate the *real* Gospel in a light that can be understood.

> **Genesis 28:13-14**—. . . I *am* the Lord God of Abraham thy father, and the God of Isaac: the land whereon thou liest, to thee will I give it, and to thy seed; And thy seed shall be as the dust of the earth, and thou shalt spread abroad to the west, and to the east, and to the north, and to the south: and in thee and in thy seed shall all the families of the earth be blessed.

So, through Jacob, son of Isaac, son of Abraham, would the *seed* be given that would bless all the families of the earth.

> **Galatians 3:16, 29**—Now to Abraham and his seed were the promises made . . . which is Christ . . . And if ye *be* Christ's; then are ye Abraham's seed, and heirs according to the promise.

> **Galatians 3:26-28**—For ye are all the children of God by faith in Christ Jesus. For as many of you as have been baptized into Christ have put on Christ. There is neither Jew nor Greek, there is neither bond nor free, there is neither male nor female: for ye are all one in Christ Jesus.

We are all one in Christ Jesus, (one with the Jews), and

have received every blessing and promise ever made by God concerning His children or Jesus concerning His brethren. The Gentile *that is saved* in the present age is Abraham's seed because he is in Christ Jesus.

As declared in Psalms 105, the covenant was to be renewed with Isaac, Jacob and the Israelites from generation to generation. It also came with the warning to Abraham stated in Genesis 17:7,". . . to be a God unto thee, and to thy seed after thee."

Many are hurt, jealous, even envious because God chose Israel to receive all the good things that He has to bestow upon His elect. But are they, the remaining natural seed of Israel, the Seed of Promise? Has God really bestowed His blessings on them as a nation? No! Not since King Nebuchadnezzar took Israel captive, has God bestowed any unmerited favors, except one—*Jesus*—whom the Jews, as a nation, rejected.

> **John 3:16**—For God so loved the world, that He gave His only begotten Son, that whosoever believeth in Him should not perish, but have everlasting life.

So why do so many people feel the way they do about Israel? I recall one dear friend who was hurt beyond measure because she thought it was unfair of God to give Israel all good things and for Him to bestow His favors as if He were the Teacher and they were the Teacher's pets—pets, because of their nationality. She truly believed that God cared more for Israel than for any other nation and that He cared more for a Jew than others. This way of thinking is a total misconception of God's Word—a gross misinterpretation of the Scriptures.

17

> **Romans 2:11**—For there is no respect of
> persons with God.

God does not show respect for one's good looks, one's
nationality, the color of one's skin, or whether one is male or
female, Jew or Greek, bond or free, Israelite or American.
Only man shows respect, and hates for these reasons.

We should not allow the idea that God has favorites to
enter into our mind. Remember, the only reason salvation
was delivered to the Jews first was because they were the
only nation to serve and believe in the God of Abraham.

> **Acts 1:8**—But ye shall receive power, af-
> ter that the Holy Ghost is come upon you:
> and ye shall be witnesses unto Me both in
> Jerusalem, and in all Judaea, and in
> Samaria, and unto the uttermost part of the
> earth.

Yes, Jesus commissioned the first church, made up of
believing Jews, to take the Gospel to the uttermost parts of
the earth. The Jews however, having failed their commis-
sion, have passed that task on to the current church—a church
made up of every nationality and race. Proof once more that
God is not a respecter of persons.

Anyone not of the church, whether Jew or Gentile, who
rejects Jesus will, if alive at the time of the rapture, *go through
the tribulation.* Does this sound like God is being partial?

*Why has Israel always been sold into slavery, persecuted
and afflicted by the heathen? Will it never change? Will God
ever fulfill His promise to Abraham?* These, and other questions, will be answered as we study the Word.

The government of the Millennial Kingdom will be made
up of the people in Christ:

18

> **Isaiah 9:6**—. . . the government will be
> upon His shoulders . . .

> **Revelation 20:6**—. . . but they shall be
> "priests of God and of Christ" and shall
> reign with Him . . .

Only those who have part in the first resurrection will reign with Him. There should not be, nor will there be, any politics in this government for it will be neither political or spiritual where one nation or people has preeminence or power over another. It will be a government obedient to Him.

From the time of Christ until the Second World War when Hitler killed one-third of the world's Jewish population, the Israelite nation decayed and degenerated. It was not until 1948 that Israel came into being and was recognized as a nation.

Israel lost the Holy City to the Islamic regime centuries ago and, even today, the Dome of the Islam god stands on the very site of Solomon's Temple—the Temple that was to have remained forever.

Is Abraham the blessed? Is Abraham the blesser? Are the families blessed of Abraham? Are the families blessed by the nation Israel? Is the nation Israel blessed? Each of these questions is pertinent; however, if they serve God, in Christ, no nation is blessed above any other nation. Scripture tells us that *all families* are blessed, families being nations:

> **Genesis 28:14**—And thy seed shall be as
> the dust of the earth, and thou shalt spread
> abroad to the west, and to the east, and to
> the north, and to the south: and in thee and
> in thy seed shall all the families of the earth
> be blessed.

19

Today we see those nations that are serving God being blessed more than the nations that serve false gods.

Israel will not rebuild the Temple on the Holy Grounds until after the rapture. The abomination of desolation spoken of by the prophet Daniel in Daniel 9:27 and 12:11 is now standing in the Holy Place. There are two reasons why the temple will not be rebuilt: One: The old covenant and temple cannot replace Jesus, who died once for all; otherwise, He died in vain. Two: If, and it's a big if, Israel reclaimed the Holy City and the Holy Grounds and rebuilt Solomon's Temple, would they then count these gains as nothing—things of no value—and turn to Christ? Not so!

This is, at best, a very weak presumption and would only reaffirm to the Jewish people that Jesus was a "good man," but not the Messiah—the Seed of Promise! They would continue to look for another as their promised Messiah!

The Jews will not come to believe in Jesus until the seven years of tribulation. Until then, they will believe in the Roman prince they have found as their long-hoped-for King. Most theologians agree that the Roman Prince is the Anti-Christ. This Prince will make, and later break, a covenant with Israel. If those who follow the Anti-Christ have taken the mark of the Beast, how then can they be saved? There is only one way—they must reject the Anti-Christ and believe in Jesus!

> **Revelations 13:8**—And all that dwell upon the earth shall worship him, whose names are not written in the Book of Life of the Lamb . . .

> **Galatians 3:14-18 and 26-29**—That the blessing of Abraham might come on the Gentiles through Jesus Christ; that we might receive the promise of the Spirit

through faith. Brethren, I speak after the manner of men; Though *it be* but a man's covenant, yet *if it be* confirmed, no man disannulleth, or addeth thereto. Now to Abraham and his seed were the promises made. He saith not, And to seeds, as of many; but as of one, And to thy seed, which is Christ. And this I say, *that* the covenant that was confirmed before of God in Christ, the law, which was four hundred and thirty years after, cannot disannul, that it should make the promise of none effect. For if the inheritance *be* of the law, *it is* no more of promise; but God gave *it* to Abraham by promise.

For ye are all the children of God by faith in Christ Jesus. For as many of you as have been baptized into Christ have put on Christ. There is neither Jew nor Greek, there is neither bond nor free, there is neither male nor female: for ye are all one in Christ Jesus. And if ye *be* Christ's, then are ye Abraham's seed, and heirs according to the promise.

Christ is the Seed, not according to law or inheritance, but the Seed promised to Abraham by God.

If we are the children of God by faith in Jesus then we are Abraham's seed and heirs to the promise. Heirs to the promise, not according to flesh or the birth-right of nationality, but heirs in Christ. If this is not so, then His life and death become meaningless. The Jewish law would be right, taking away any chance for a Gentile to be saved. The Cross of Jesus would have no effect on our salvation because salvation could only come to us through inheritance. Many church members today have inherited their religion, even their church membership, and have left Christ's salvation plan completely out of their faith. They forget that Jesus was, and is, "The Seed of Promise" promised to David in Second Samuel 7:16 and to Solomon in First Kings 9:5.

CHAPTER TWO

THE PROMISE TO THE CHOSEN

"We, the Chosen Frozen Few," is a phrase sometimes used to describe the mannerisms of different churches. It could also be used to describe the attitude that some have when they talk about the Israelite nation being the permanent chosen of God.

God chose the Israelites as His people because they were the only people who believed in the God of Abraham, Isaac and Jacob. He could not be the god of the Baal worshippers, or the worshippers of the Greek gods Astarte, Asherah, Baalzebub, Bel, Dagon, Jupiter, Diana, Mercury, Nebo, Satyr, Caster, just to name a few.

Common sense alone should dictate that God could not appear as the god of a pagan nation. In Exodus 20:3 He said, "Thou shalt have no other gods before Me." He will not be second to any. Jesus could not have been born into an American Indian family. *Why?* Because the Indian people worshiped the god of wind, the god of rain, and other false gods. The Indian people didn't learn about the Great White Father and the Great Spirit until after the Pilgrims landed at Plymouth Rock. In the west and southwest, the Word was brought to them by Spanish monks and priests that came up from Mexico. Before this, they had never heard of God.

Jesus could not have been born into a heathen nation. No, He had to be born into the Israel nation, the only nation that could accept Him as Savior. Born there, not because the Israelites were God's chosen, but because they were Abraham's descendents and heir to the promise. They were the only people who knew of and had chosen God. Today, God's chosen are not determined by nationality, good looks, social standing, riches, or any other course. God's chosen are those who come to Him through Jesus and ask to be chosen.

When we choose Jesus, the only begotten Son of God, then God chooses to accept us. *Why?* Because we have accepted the Blood of Jesus, spilled on Calvary, as our source of redemption and salvation. Do you, my Jewish friends, wish to be chosen His way by Jesus' Blood, or by birth? Choose to be "born again" in Jesus—the only way to Heaven!

> **Numbers 16:5**—And he spake unto Korah and unto all his company, saying, Even tomorrow the Lord will shew who *are* His, and *who is* holy; and will cause him to come near unto Him: even *him* whom He hath chosen will He cause to come near unto Him.

> **Numbers 16:21, 30, 32**—Separate yourselves from among this congregation, that I may consume them in a moment . . . But if the Lord make a new thing, and the earth open her mouth, and swallow them up, with all that *appertain* unto them, and they go down quick into the pit; then ye shall understand that these men have provoked the Lord . . . And the earth opened her mouth,

> and swallowed them up, and their houses,
> and all the men that *appertained* unto
> Korah, and all *their* goods.

Moses spoke unto Korah and all his company, which was his entire house, warning them that tomorrow the Lord would separate the chosen from among His people.

We know that Korah and his descendants were children of Israel, but not God's chosen. How do we know this? Because He caused the earth to open and swallow up the entire family in an earthquake. This was God's way of separating the chosen out of the congregation.

The covenant God made with Abraham, Isaac, Jacob, David, and Solomon, although made with individuals, affected the entire nation of Israel. We should thank God that He no longer deals with nations, but with individuals! Isaiah 43:9 says, "Let all the nations be gathered together . . ." And they will! During the Millennium, all nations will become one, one people under one rule—Christ!

> **Isaiah 43:20-22**—My people, My chosen.
> This people have I formed for Myself: they
> shall shew forth My praise. But thou hast
> not called upon Me, O Jacob: but thou hast
> been weary of Me O Israel . . .

This Scripture clearly declares that Jacob (Israel) is not to be the chosen. *Who then are the chosen? All* people of *all* nations that are in Christ—they are the chosen!.

> **Isaiah 43:25-28**—. . . I, *even* I, *am* He that
> blotteth out thy transgressions for mine own
> sake, and will not remember thy sins. Put
> Me in remembrance: let us plead together:
> declare thou, that thou mayest be justified.

Thy first father hath sinned, and thy teach-
ers have transgressed against Me. Therefore I have profaned the princes of the sanc-
tuary, and have given Jacob the curse, and
Israel to reproaches.

Yes, if they are justified, God has blotted out their transgressions and the descendants of Israel are the chosen. He
does so, however, only if they are regenerated individuals.
Why? Because, on the whole, the nation—Jacob to the curse
and Israel to reproaches—have been cut off! Only the regenerated are the chosen—chosen the same way we are—by coming to God through Christ.

Isaiah 44:21-22—Remember these, O
Jacob and Israel; for thou *art* My servant:
I have formed thee; thou *art* My servant:
O Israel, thou shalt not be forgotten of Me.
I have blotted out, as a thick cloud, thy
transgressions, and, as a cloud, thy sins:
return unto Me; for I have redeemed thee.

To be redeemed, they have to return to God, through
Christ!

I Peter 1:2—Elect according to the fore-
knowledge of God the Father, through sanc-
tification of the Spirit, unto obedience and
sprinkling of the Blood of Jesus Christ . . .

I Peter 2:9—But ye *are* a chosen generation, a royal priesthood, an holy nation, a
peculiar people; that ye should shew forth
the praises of Him who hath called you out

of darkness into His marvellous light:

Peter wrote these words to the strangers scattered throughout Pontus, Galatia, Cappadocia, Asia and Bithynia telling them that they were a chosen generation, obedient and sprinkled with the Blood of Jesus Christ. *Hello!* Sprinkled with the Blood of Jesus! Are all the Israelites followers of Jesus? No! Then the chosen must be, and have to be, born again by the Blood of Jesus! *How then do some claim that all Israelites are chosen, when most do not believe in or accept Jesus?* Yes, Peter was a Jew, but he was also a follower of Jesus!

> **Revelation 7:9 and 14b**—After this I beheld, and, lo, a great multitude, which no man could number, of all nations, and kindreds, and people, and tongues, stood before the Throne, and before the Lamb, clothed with white robes, and palms in their hands . . . These are they which came out of great tribulation, and have washed their robes, and made them white in the Blood of the Lamb.

> **Revelation 17:14**—. . . for He is Lord of Lords, and King of Kings: and they that are with Him *are* called, and chosen, and faithful.

The chosen are of all nations, kindreds, people and tongues. God, in Acts 9:15 calls Paul "A chosen vessel unto Me." And Jesus, in Acts 1:2 tells us that He, through the Holy Ghost gave "commands unto the apostles whom He had chosen." *Chosen out of a chosen people? Double talk?* No!

Before Christ came, the Israelites were the chosen; now, whosoever will, may come and be chosen!

CHAPTER THREE

THE PROMISE TO THE ELECT

The prophesies concerning the nations at the end of time are true. One can see by the current events that those prophesies are being fulfilled. While it is good to stay knowledgeable on current events, it is better to know God's divine will. It is not God's will that any should perish, but that *all* should come to repentance.

> **II Peter 3:9**—The Lord is not slack concerning His promise, as some men count slackness; but is longsuffering to us-ward, not willing that any should perish, but that all should come to repentance.

One might say, "But this was written to the Church of the New Testament and not to the Jews." But, look again, what does the Scripture say? "That *all* should come to repentance." *All* means *all*—that includes the Jews.

> **II Peter 1:1**—Simon Peter, a servant and an apostle of Jesus Christ, to them that have

29

obtained like precious faith with us through
the righteousness of God and our Savior,
Jesus Christ:

This Scripture was written to all who had obtained their
faith through Jesus! This does not pertain to the Jew who has
chosen Jesus as Savior, nor does it pertain to the nation of
Israel today. It does not apply to a group of people or a nation—only to those saved by the Blood of Jesus.

> **I Peter 1:1-2**—Peter, an apostle of Jesus
> Christ, to the strangers scattered through-
> out Pontus, Galatia, Cappadocia, Asia, and
> Bithynia. Elect according to the foreknowl-
> edge of God the Father, through sanctifica-
> tion of the Spirit, unto obedience and sprin-
> kling of the Blood of Jesus Christ: Grace
> unto you, and peace, be multiplied.

The *elect* are blood-bought by Jesus, not by the birth-
right of Abraham's covenant. All of the strangers are elect!
The elect were also the saved Jews, the ones who believed in
Jesus who were scattered abroad. This applied *only* to the
Jews in Christ and not the entire Jewish nation. This Gospel
was, and is, for the Jew who is saved in Jesus and those who
will be saved in Jesus.

> **Hosea 1:7**—But I will have mercy upon
> the house of Judah, and will not save them
> by bow, nor by sword, nor by battle, by
> horses, nor by horsemen.

God said He would save Judah—not Israel. Today, both
Israel and Judah are waiting to be saved by a big battle or
war. They wait in anticipation for a great messiah-leader that

will restore to them the entire Abraham land covenant, including Jerusalem, and who will rebuild their temple in place of the Islamic dome. *How wrong can they be?*

> **Hosea 7:1, 2, 14, 16**—When I would have healed Israel, then the iniquity of Ephraim was discovered, and the wickedness of Samaria: for they commit falsehood; and the thief cometh in, *and* the troop of robbers spoileth without. And they consider not in their hearts *that* I remember all their wickedness: now their own doings have beset them about; they are before my face . . . And they have not cried unto me with their heart, when they howled upon their beds: they assemble themselves for corn and wine, *and* they rebel against Me . . . They return, *but* not to the Most High: they are like a deceitful bow: their princes shall fall by the sword for the rage of their tongue: this *shall* be their derision in the land of Egypt.

Israel returns to Israel, but not to the Most High. Today, they are returning to their land; however, they are not returning to God. And, the only way they can return to Him is through His Son, Christ Jesus.

> **Matthew 24:24**—For there shall arise false Christs, and false prophets, and shall shew great signs and wonders; insomuch that, if it *were* possible, they shall deceive the very elect.

In Scripture, the "elect" are also sometimes referred to

31

as the "called." Romans 8:28 is an example of this, ". . . who are *called* according to His purpose."

> **I Peter 1:3-5**—Blessed *be* the God and Father of our Lord Jesus Christ, which according to His abundant mercy hath begotten us again unto a lively hope by the resurrection of Jesus Christ from the dead. To an inheritance incorruptible, and undefiled, and that fadeth not away, reserved in Heaven for you, Who are kept by the power of God through faith unto salvation ready to be revealed in the last time.

First Peter 1:2 tells us that the elect must be born again of the Spirit, washed in the Blood of Jesus Christ, sanctified in the Spirit, obedient and kept by the power of God. This will not include the Jew who has not been bought by the redeeming Blood of Jesus! As most Israelites do not believe in Jesus, they cannot be the elect!

> **I Corinthians 12:12-13**—For as the body is one, and hath many members, and all the members of that one body, being many, are one body: so also *is* Christ. For by one Spirit are we all baptized into one body, whether *we be* Jews or Gentiles, whether *we be* bond or free; and have been all made to drink into one Spirit.

The Jew and Gentile alike who are of the Body of Christ *are the elect*! Peter, in I Peter 1:1, called the strangers *"the elect,"* as did Isaiah:

> **Isaiah 45:4**—For Jacob My servant's sake,

32

and Israel Mine elect, I have even called
thee by thy name: I have surnamed thee,
though thou hast not known Me.

Until Jesus was crucified, the Israelites were the only
people God had. But now, through Jesus, the Gentiles can
become the elect—one body with the Jew!

But what about Mary's ancestors? We know that through
her there were Gentile ancestors to Jesus. And, what about
the many Gentiles of Egypt who married people of Israel and
became Jews? Their children became "Children of Israel,"
and were counted as Israelites! In this manner many became
children of God and were counted as the elect. We also know
that many people of the land became Jews "for fear of the
Jews."

> **Esther 8:17**—And in every province, and
> in every city, withersoever the king's com-
> mandment and his decree came, the Jews
> had joy and gladness, a feast and a good
> day. And many of the people of the land
> became Jews; for the fear of the Jews fell
> upon them.

We are told in Esther 1:1 that the people of the land included all nations under King Ahesuerus, "from India even
unto Ethiopia, one hundred and seven and twenty provinces."
People of many languages and nations were there.

So the elect are God's people, but only in Christ, His
Son. This elect does not include pagan, heathen, or those
who reject Christ, whether Jew or Gentile.

Paul, in Romans 8:33, called the Romans, "God's elect."
And, in Colossians 3:2, he called the Colossians "the elect of
God." In Colossians 3:17, he said, "Whatsoever ye do, in

word or deed, do all in the name of the Lord Jesus . . ."

> **Acts 13:26**—Men *and* brethren, children
> of the stock of Abraham, and whosoever
> among you feareth God, to you is the word
> of this salvation sent.

First to the Jew, and then to the Gentile. Let us look at the Old Testament—God's Word to Israel:

> **Deuteronomy 8:19-20**—And it shall be,
> if thou do at all forget the Lord thy God,
> and walk after other gods, and serve them,
> and worship them, I testify against you this
> day that ye shall surely perish. As the na-
> tions which the Lord destroyeth before your
> face, so shall ye perish; because ye would
> not be obedient unto the voice of the Lord
> your God.

> **II Chronicles 7:14**—If My people, which
> are called by My name, shall humble them-
> selves, and pray, and seek My face, and turn
> from their wicked ways; then will I hear
> from Heaven, and will forgive their sin, and
> will heal their land.

God said to obey and repent. If the Jew disobeyed, he had to repent and turn from his wicked ways, or perish. Except they repent, they would not go into the Promised Land or the Millennium.

Many ministers of God's Word do not know that the meaning of "repent" is the turning away from one's wicked ways! In the 6th chapter of Genesis, God repented that He had made man. He not only turned from wicked man, but He got rid of the very thing He was repenting of—man. When man repents, he, too, must get rid of the very thing he is repenting of or he has not truly repented.

Saved by grace? Yes! *Saved in one's sins?* God forbid! *Once saved, always saved?* No! Not saved to continue in to sin! When one sins, they must repent, turn from their wicked ways, and come back to God! Neither are the Jews, just because they are Jews, saved. Neither, while they are in their sins, are they God's chosen. Jesus, in John 8:44 said, "Ye are of your father, the Devil . . ."

> **Isaiah 45:25**—In the Lord shall all the seed of Israel be justified, and shall glory.

"In the Lord shall all the seed of Israel be *justified.*" Not by the seed are they justified, not by works are they justified, not by Abraham or his covenant with God are they justified. They are justified only in the Lord and through obedience to His Word.

> **Matthew 24:31**—And He shall send His angels with a great sound of a trumpet, and they shall gather His elect from the four winds, from one end of Heaven to the other.

After the tribulation, according to Matthew 24:29, Jesus will send His angels to gather His elect. The elect is the bride, the raptured church. *My friend, will you be a part of that number?*

35

CHAPTER FOUR

THE PROMISE TO THE REMNANT

> **Romans 11:5, 7**—. . . there is a remnant according to the election of grace . . . What then? Israel hath not obtained that which he seeketh for; but the election hath obtained it, and the rest were blinded.

The remnant of believers are the elect. Israelites, on the whole, have not been saved; however, a remnant have. It is this remnant that is the elect! Likewise, only a remnant of gentiles are of the elect! Who then, is the elect? All in Christ that repent—both Jew and Gentile—are the elect!

> **Romans 4:16**—Therefore *it is* of faith, that *it might be* by grace; to the end the promise might be sure to all the seed; not to that only which is of the law, but to that also which is of the faith of Abraham; who is the father of us all.

This was written to the Roman Gentiles. The promise is to *all* by faith!

Jeremiah 3:14—Turn, o backsliding children, saith the Lord; for I am married unto you: and I will take you one of a city, and two of a family, and I will bring you to Zion.

One of a city and two of a family is a remnant. God will not take all of Israel—only those who turn back to Him.

Colossians 3:11-12—Where there is neither Greek nor Jew, circumcision nor uncircumcision, Barbarian, Scythian, bond, *nor* free: but Christ is all, and in all. Put on therefore, as the elect of God, holy and beloved . . .

The elect of God takes in *all* of the remnant that are in Christ. Jesus, Himself said:

Luke 13:3—I tell you, Nay: but, except ye repent, ye shall all likewise perish.

It is the Jews who have always fought the Gospel! It was the Jews who rebelled against Moses and the prophets. It was the Jews who rebelled against Jesus and denied Him. It was the Jews who stoned Paul and left him for dead. But the elect, the remnant, were saved! God has always had a remnant!

If the un-regenerate, un-repentant Jew can be saved at the end of time only because they are a Jew, then all generations of Jews in the past will also be saved, no matter how rebellious they were!

Daniel 12:1—And at that time shall Michael stand up, the great prince which

standeth for the children of Thy people: and
there shall be a time of trouble, such as
never was since there was a nation even to
that same time: and at that time Thy people
shall be delivered, every one that shall be
found written in the Book.

Only His people that are *written in the book* shall be
delivered!

Exodus 32:33—And the Lord said unto
Moses, Whosoever hath sinned against Me,
him will I blot out of My Book.

Whoever has sinned, God will blot out!!

How does this compare to Romans 11:26 where Paul
writes, "And so all Israel shall be saved . . ." If taken out of
context, this statement would contradict the rest of the Bible.
Let's look at the essence of the entire eleventh chapter.

Romans 11:23—If they abide not still in
unbelief, shall be graffed in: for God is
able to graff them in again.

And so all Israel shall be saved, after they are graffed in.

Isaiah 59:20—And the Redeemer shall
come to Zion, and unto them that turn from
transgression in Jacob, saith the Lord.

Only those who turn from their transgressions and repent shall be saved.

Romans 11:5-7—Even so then at this
present time also there is a remnant accord-

38

ing to the election of grace . . . What then?
Israel hath not obtained that which he
seeketh for; but the election hath obtained
it, and the rest were blinded.

Not of the race—but of the election of grace. Not of
Abraham—but of the *I AM*. Those who believe are saved by
grace, the rest are blinded! Let us not add to that blindness!
We know by what it says in Romans 11:23 that *if* they believe, accept Jesus, and are born-again, God is able to graff
them in again. Then, He will take them back once more!

II Chronicles 7:14—If My people, which
are called by My name, shall humble themselves, and pray, and seek My face, and turn
from their wicked ways; then will I hear
from Heaven, and will forgive their sin, and
will heal their land.

Jesus, in John 3:3, said to the Jews, ". . . Except a man
be born again, he cannot see the Kingdom of God." They
must be born again, and not just born a Jew!

II Chronicles 34:9—And when they came
to Hilkiah the high priest, they delivered
the money that was brought into the House
of God, which the Levites that kept the
doors had gathered of the hand of Manasseh
and Ephraim, and of all the remnant of Israel, and of all Judah and Benjamin; and
they returned to Jerusalem.

Isaiah 46:3—Hearken unto Me, O house
of Jacob, and all the remnant of the house

39

of Israel, which are borne by *Me* from the
belly, which are carried from the womb:

Isaiah 46:13—I bring near My righteousness: it shall not be far off, and My salvation shall not tarry: and I will place salvation in Zion for Israel my glory.

The remnant of Israel did return to Jerusalem and they
did repair the house of God.

God promised salvation to the remnant of Israel if they
would but hearken unto Him. God's promise was that He
would place His salvation in Zion, which He did. He sent
His Son, Jesus, to be born in a manger in Bethlehem, not only
for Israel, but for the world. Israel, however, on the whole,
did not recognize Him as their salvation. Only a remnant
believed. A remnant that became the foundation of the New
Testament Church.

This remnant, along with the disobedient of Israel, has
suffered. *Why?* Here is an example: God blesses one person
in a household, yet the entire house receives the same blessing. This causes the disobedient to think, *my sin is the per-
missive will of God, look how He blesses me.* However, when
God, because of their disobedience, chooses not to bless the
entire family, the person in the household who is trying to
serve God does not receive the blessing either. That person
has a hard time living faithfully. In time, however; because of
their obedience, they will reap their reward.

Jeremiah 42:2, 3—And said unto Jeremiah
the prophet, Let, we beseech thee, our supplication be accepted before thee, and pray
for us unto the Lord thy God, *even* for all
this remnant, (for we are left *but* a few of
many, as thine eyes do behold us:) That

the Lord thy God may shew us the way wherein we may walk, and the thing that we may do.

Jeremiah 42:9, 10, 13—Thus saith the Lord, the God of Israel, unto whom ye sent me to present your supplication before Him; If ye will still abide in this land, then will I build you, and not pull *you* down, and I will plant you, and not pluck *you* up: . . . But if ye say, We will not dwell in this land, neither obey the voice of the Lord your God.

Jeremiah 42:15, 16—And now therefore hear the word of the Lord, ye remnant of Judah; Thus saith the Lord of Hosts, the God of Israel; If ye wholly set your faces to enter into Egypt, and go to sojourn there; Then it shall come to pass, *that* the sword, which ye feared, shall overtake you there in the land of Egypt, and the famine, whereof ye were afraid, shall follow close after you there in Egypt; and there ye shall die.

Jeremiah 43:2, 7—Then spake, Azariah the son of Hoshaiah, and Johnanan the son of Kareah, and all the proud men, saying unto Jeremiah, Thou speakest falsely: The Lord our God hath not sent thee to say, Go not into Egypt to sojourn there: . . . So they came into the land of Egypt: for they obeyed not the voice of the Lord: . . .

Jeremiah 44:2—Thus saith the Lord of Hosts, the God of Israel; Ye have seen all

the evil that I have brought upon Jerusalem, and upon all the cities of Judah; and,
behold, this day they *are* a desolation, and
no man dwelleth therein.

Jeremiah 44:28—Yet a small number that
escape the sword shall return out of the land
of Egypt into the land of Judah, and all the
remnant of Judah, that are gone into the land
of Egypt to sojourn there, shall know whose
words shall stand, Mine, or theirs.

So we see that the remnant have been destroyed time
after time because of their disobedience, but, there are always a few that escape destruction. It is these few who God
remembers, blesses, and nurtures back to health. That is, until
the next generation of unbelievers once more provoke His
anger.

Jeremiah went with the remnant of Judah, however, he
did not receive a blessing because the remnant of Judah could
not be blessed! He received his reward and is in Heaven
because of his faithfulness to God. The disobedient will go
to Heaven because of their blood line? *Don't kid yourself!*
God is no respecter of person, nation, Jew or Gentile. He
has always demanded obedience and always will! Can we
not see this? Azariah accused Jeremiah of being a false
prophet and persuaded the people not to hearken unto God.
Today, there are still false prophets in the world teaching things
they should not be teaching. Many people blindly follow these
leaders into perdition. Often, it seems that the false prophets
attract a larger following than a man of God! But, don't be
deceived!

God will have a remnant! One lady came to our church
only when she wanted prayer. When asked one Sunday morn-
ing if she would like to return that night for the evening ser-

vice, she gave the excuse that she couldn't drive at night. We offered to have someone drive to her home and pick her up but she declined, saying that she and her husband attended another church on Sunday night.

Shortly thereafter, I happened to see her husband while I was out shopping. We spoke for a few minutes and in the course of our conversation I invited him to our church. He politely refused stating that he was established in another church. He went on to tell me how much his wife enjoyed coming to our church and finished by saying that she had her own car and was free to come at any time, day or night.

About six months after our discussion, this man accidently met his death at his workplace. God had removed the disobedient child's excuse. Needless to say, except for coming in for prayer from time to time, his wife never returned to our church.

In the course of my ministry I have learned not to remove a person's excuse. If they are going to obey—they will. And, if they are not going to obey—they won't. They will not hearken to my voice or even to the voice of God.

> **Revelation 12:17**—And the dragon was wroth with the woman, and went to make war with the remnant of her seed, which keep the Commandments of God, and have testimony of Jesus Christ.

The woman in this Scripture is the church of today. The Devil is mad at the church. Revelation 12:5 tells us that she gave birth to Jesus: ". . . Her Child was caught up unto God and to His Throne." Revelation 12:9 informs us that the ". . . Devil was cast out upon the earth."

Today, the Dragon, another name for the Devil, is making war against the remnant of the seed who are keeping God's

Commandments and who have the testimony of Jesus Christ. Note that it is *seed* (singular) and not *seeds* (plural). Jesus is singular not plural!

So the remnant of Israel is the church of today. The people of Israel, without Jesus, are *not* the remnant!

CHAPTER FIVE

THE PROMISE TO THE BRETHREN

Matthew 25:31-46—When the Son of Man shall come in His glory, and all the holy angels with Him, then shall He sit upon the throne of His glory: And before Him shall be gathered <u>all nations</u>: and He shall separate them one from another, as a shepherd divideth *his* sheep from the goats: And He shall set the sheep on His right hand, but the goats on the left. Then shall the King say unto them on His right hand, Come, ye blessed of My Father, inherit the Kingdom prepared for you from the foundation of the world: For I was an hungered, and ye gave Me meat: I was thirsty, and ye gave Me drink: I was a stranger, and ye took Me in: Naked, and ye clothed Me: I was sick, and ye visited Me: I was in prison, and ye came unto Me. Then shall the righteous answer Him, saying, Lord, when saw we Thee an hungered, and fed *Thee*? Or thirsty, and gave *Thee* drink?

When saw we Thee a stranger, and took *Thee* in? Or naked, and clothed *Thee*? Or when saw we Thee sick, or in prison, and came unto Thee? And the King shall answer and say unto them, Verily I say unto you, inasmuch as ye have done *it* unto one of the least of these My brethren, ye have done *it* unto Me.

Then shall He say also unto them on the left hand, Depart from Me, ye cursed, into everlasting fire, prepared for the Devil and his angels: For I was an hungered, and ye gave Me no meat: I was thirsty, and ye gave Me no drink: I was a stranger, and ye took Me not in: naked, and ye clothed Me not: sick, and in prison, and ye visited Me not. Then shall they also answer Him, saying, Lord, when saw we Thee an hungered, or athirst, or a stranger, or naked, or sick, or in prison, and did not minister unto Thee? Then shall He answer them, saying, Verily I say unto you, Inasmuch as ye did *it* not to one of the least of these, ye did *it* not to Me. And these shall go away into everlasting punishment: but the righteous into life eternal.

This clearly states that the subjects are "all nations!" I believe that the Jewish nation and people are included in this judgment and will be separated with the sheep and goats, leaving the "brethren" to come from all nations.

Jesus will be sitting on His throne. All nations, including Israel, will be there. Every person will be separated by Jesus from their nation and be judged according to how they have treated His brethren. The sheep He will place on His right hand, and the goats on the left.

This is the judgment for entrance into the Millennial Kingdom. *Who will be judged?* Everyone alive at the end of the tribulation. *All* people of every nation, including Israel will be judged on the way they have treated Jesus' brethren. This includes the "brethren" who have already passed into Heaven via the rapture.

Who are the brethren? Jesus, in Matthew 12:50, said, "For whosoever shall do the will of My Father which is in Heaven, the same is my brother, and sister, and mother." And Paul, in Romans 12:1, called the Gentile Romans "brethren." Therefore, all that are of Christ are His brethren.

Who are the sheep? The sheep are those who took the brethren in, fed them, gave them to drink, clothed them, and visited them in prison.

Who are the goats? The goats are those who saw Christ's brethren hungry, thirsty, naked, sick, or in prison, and did nothing .

> **Leviticus 19:35-37**—Ye shall do no unrighteousness in judgment, in meteyard, in weight, or in measure. Just balances, just weights, a just ephah, and a just hin, shall ye have: I *am* the Lord your God, which brought you out of the land of Egypt. Therefore shall ye observe all My statutes, and all My judgment, and do them: I *am* the Lord.

This, of course, is exactly what has taken place. For over 2500 years the Israelites have had no country of their own.

> **Amos 8:2, 4-5**—And He said, Amos, what seest thou? And I said, A basket of sum-

mer fruit. Then said the Lord unto me, The end is come upon My people of Israel; I will not again pass by them any more . . . Hear this, O ye that swallow up the needy, even to make the poor of the land to fail, Saying, When will the new moon be gone, that we may sell corn? and the sabbath, that we may set forth wheat, making the ephah small, and the shekel great, and falsifying the balances by deceit?

I have seen Jewish businessmen, as well as men from other nationalities, falsify their scales and overprice their goods, thereby cheating some of God's people and enabling themselves to become rich. Many of those who have been cheated become angry and hate the Jews because of their business tactics! In Amos 8:2 God said, ". . . The end is come upon My people of Israel; I will not again pass by them any more . . ." They have cheated their own people as well. Some Israelites will be separated with the goats! Not all of Israel will enter the Millennial Kingdom!

All, for the purpose of entering into the Millennial, will be judged according to their works. But my Jewish friends, wouldn't it be better to be with Paul, Peter, and John, and make the rapture?

In Matthew 12:49, Jesus pointed to His disciples and said, "Behold My mother and My brethren!" Jesus also called His disciples, "His brethren."

If we assume all Jews to be Jesus' "brethren," then only those who were present with Him could be His brethren. This erroneous interpretation would limit the end-time message solely to His disciples and those who came in contact with the disciples. A broader, more sound, interpretation is stated by Jesus, Himself.

48

> **Matthew 18:2,6 and Luke 17:2**—Jesus
> called a little child unto Him and set him in
> the midst of them . . . And He said, Verily
> I say unto you, Except, ye be converted,
> and become as little children, ye shall not
> enter into the Kingdom of Heaven. Who-
> soever therefore shall humble this little
> child, the same is greatest in the Kingdom
> of Heaven and whosoever shall receive one
> such little child in My name receiveth me.
> But whoso shall offend one of these little
> ones which believe in Me, it were better
> for him, that a millstone were hanged about
> his neck, and *that* he were drowned in the
> depth of the sea.

So the judgment would include any person who had mis-
treated *any* little one who believes in Jesus! Remember, it
was Jesus who was speaking—for the little ones to be counted
by Him as brethren, they would have to believe in Him. And,
on the whole, the Jewish people do not believe in or accept
Christ! This, of course, does not mean that some will not be
saved during the Millennium. These, too, will be counted as
"brethren" and will be separated with the sheep.

> **I Corinthians 12:12**—For as the body is
> one, and hath many members, and all the
> members of that one body, being many, are
> one body: so also *is* Christ.

The Church of Corinth was made up of Gentiles, yet
Paul called them "brethren." These Gentiles had worshiped
idols or false gods, but they had also heard the Gospel and
some were saved. *How many were saved?* Only God knows!

49

We find that fornication, wild fire, jealousy, and church bickering were common in the Church at Corinth.

Paul, in First Corinthians 11:21, 22, rebuked the church for gluttony and for using the church for social gatherings. This denotes that it was a carnal, rather than a spiritual church. God's church is spiritual—a spiritual church made up of all nationalities and all denominations. A church where the members refer to each other as "brethren."

> **II Corinthians 3:13-15**—... that the children of Israel could not steadfastly look to the end of that which is abolished: But their minds were blinded: for until this day remaineth the same vail untaken away in the reading of the Old Testament; which vail is done away in Christ. But even unto this day, when Moses is read, the vail is upon their heart. Nevertheless when it shall turn to the Lord, the vail shall be taken away.

Today, many Jewish people are blinded to the truth. And, those who believe the Jewish people to be *the chosen* are also blinded—blinded by the reading of the Old Testament, which was abolished by Jesus. *What part of the Old Testament did He abolish?* The ten commandments? The prophets? The Law? Hear now, you who are blind, the entire Old Testament including the promises made to Abraham, Isaac, and Jacob (Israel) is abolished—done away with in Christ and fulfilled by Jesus, the promised *seed.*

> **Ephesians 2:11-16**—Wherefore remember, that ye *being* in time past Gentiles in the flesh, who are called Uncircumcision by that which is called the Circumcision in

50

> the flesh made by hands; That at that time ye were without Christ, being aliens from the commonwealth of Israel, and strangers from the covenants of promise, having no hope, and without God in the world: But now in Christ Jesus ye who sometimes were far off are made nigh by the Blood of Christ. For He is our peace, who hath made both one, and hath broken down the middle wall of partition *between us*; Having abolished in His flesh the enmity, *even* the law of commandments *contained* in ordinances; for to make in Himself of twain one new man, *so* making peace: And that He might reconcile both unto God in one body by the Cross, having slain the enmity thereby:

The Jew and Gentile are made one in Christ, both to be in peace with one another as *brethren*. One body, one man not twain but single, one people; for Jesus abolished the law of commandments contained in ordinances, abolished it in its entirety—the whole nine yards.

> **Hebrews 7:12 and 10:28-30**—For the priesthood being changed, there is made of necessity a change also of the law . . . He that despised Moses' law died without mercy under two or three witnesses: Of how much sorer punishment, suppose ye, shall he be thought worthy, who hath trodden under foot the Son of God, and hath counted the Blood of the covenant, wherewith He was sanctified, an unholy thing, and hath done despite unto the Spirit of grace? For we know Him that hath said,

51

vengeance *belongeth* unto Me, I will rec-
ompense, saith the Lord, And again, The
Lord shall judge His people.

His people—people of grace—are God's people, but not
necessarily Israel. God will judge Israel and all who have
reelected or trodden underfoot the Son of God or have counted
His Blood as an unholy thing. You say that Israel is chosen?
Not so! *Why?* Because Israel, on the whole, has rejected
Jesus and trodden Him, and His brethren who have the spirit
of grace, underfoot.

Revelation 6:9-11—And when He had
opened the fifth seal, I saw under the altar
the souls of them that were slain for the
Word of God, and for the testimony which
they held: And they cried with a loud voice,
saying, How long, O Lord, holy and true,
dost Thou not judge and avenge our blood
on them that dwell on the earth? And white
robes were given unto every one of them;
and it was said unto them, that they should
rest yet for a little season, until their fellow
servants also and their brethren, that should
be killed as they *were*, should be fulfilled.

Many Jewish brethren have lost their lives for Jesus and
the Word of God. John 14:6 tells us that Jesus is the way, the
truth, and the life, while Revelation 19:13 identifies Him as
the Word of God! Hear Him and believe!

CHAPTER SIX

THE PROMISE TO THE HEIRS

Romans 4:12-14—And the father of circumcision to them who are not of the circumcision only, but who also walk in the steps of that faith of our father Abraham, which *he* had being yet uncircumcised. For the promise, that he should be the heir of the world, *was* not to Abraham, or to his seed, through the law, but through the righteousness of faith. For if they which are of the law *be* heirs, faith is made void, and the promise made of none effect:

Abraham, because he was not yet circumcised when he received the promise, was not living under the law covenant. The promise detailed in Genesis 17:4 was, therefore, to the heirs of the promise and not to Abram (Abraham). The heirs, are heirs by faith and not by law, or Jesus died in vain.

God promised that all the families of the earth would be

blessed as they blessed faithful Abraham. I have personally observed God bless people as they, in turn, blessed God's people. Some of those receiving God's blessing were not church people; however, because they helped Christians who were in need, God blessed them ten and even a hundred fold.

His promise surely extends to the Gentiles today—as they bless God's people, they are blessed—as they curse God's people, they are cursed. Jesus said:

> **Matthew 25:38, 40**—. . . When saw we Thee a stranger, and took *Thee* in? . . . Inasmuch as ye have done it unto one of the least of these My brethren, ye have done *it* unto Me.

Jesus also said that, regardless of nationality, we are the heirs of this promise.

> **Matthew 12:50**—For whosoever shall do the will of My Father which is in Heaven, the same is My brother, and sister, and mother.

Surely, if we can accept any promise of Scripture, we can accept these words from Paul:

> **Galatians 3:16, 29**—Now to Abraham and his seed were the promises made . . . which is Christ . . . and if ye *be* Christ's then are ye Abraham's seed, and heirs according to the promise.

I was told by a Jewish man that he would be resurrected and given a second chance. He insisted, and truly believed that he would be given 1000 years to make up his mind about

54

whether or not to accept Jesus as the Messiah. He was told this by a Gentile minister. Nowhere does the Bible teach this. This theory holds that any Jewish person or Israelite is God's chosen only because of their nationality. More on this later.

> **Romans 8:9, 13, 15, 16, 17**—But ye are not in the flesh, but in the Spirit, if so be that the Spirit of God dwell in you. Now if any man have not the Spirit of Christ, he is none of His . . . For if ye live after the flesh, ye shall die: but if ye through the Spirit do mortify the deeds of the body, ye shall live . . . For ye have not received the spirit of bondage again to fear; but ye have received the Spirit of adoption, whereby we cry, Abba, Father. The Spirit itself beareth witness with our Spirit, that we are the children of God: And if children, then heirs; heirs of God, and joint heirs with Christ. . .

Paul called the Romans who were Gentiles "heirs" through the righteousness of faith. Not heirs after the flesh, as children of Abraham, but heirs of God and joint heirs with Christ. They are the children of God—the sons of God—as promised in Galatians 3:29.

According to law, an adopted child has all the legal rights of a natural born heir. We, being adopted by the Spirit, are heirs because of the Spirit that dwells in us. In the flesh, we are not the children of Abraham; however, in the Spirit, we are the spiritual Kingdom of God. Jesus said, "My Kingdom is not of this world."

Titus 3:7, 9—That being justified by His

grace, we should be made heirs according to the hope of eternal life. But avoid foolish questions, and genealogies, and contentions, and strivings about the law; for they are unprofitable and vain.

Paul, in speaking to Titus, was telling him, and us, that we are to avoid genealogies and strivings about the law because we are justified by grace and, therefore, heirs according to the hope of eternal life.

Galatians 4:7—Wherefore thou art no more a servant, but a son; and if a son, then an heir of God through Christ.

A son, then, is an heir of God, through Christ!

There is a group of people who believe in a man-made, hearsay doctrine that falsely teaches that we, as Americans, are children of Israel. They try to prove this by genealogies and supposition. They also claim that, through Christ, we are the children of promise. All of this is supposed to entitle us to a double portion in Heaven. This teaching, of course, is patently false. First, it contains no respect of persons with God! And, we do not claim our heirship according to the flesh, but according to the Spirit of God, the Christ in us, the hope of glory!

Jesus said, "My Kingdom is not of this world." If Jesus is sitting on David's throne, then David's kingdom (Israel) is not of this world. Jesus' Kingdom is spiritual—not worldly. *If the Kingdom is spiritual, and it is, why then are we trying to restore worldly Israel to the spiritual?* Israel the nation is worldly; however, Israel the Kingdom of God is spiritual. As long as Jesus is the King of spiritual Israel, there will not be a worldly tabernacle built on the holy grounds of Jerusalem. Instead, the Mosque of the Golden Dome of the Muslim Temple of the false god of Islam will remain. This is the "abomination that maketh desolate" that Daniel spoke of in Chapter Eleven, Verse 31, of the Book that bears his name.

Emmanuel—God with us—dwells in a Tabernacle not made with hands.

He will bring the new Jerusalem with Him when He comes. In this city will be the new Temple of God.

Look up! Take your eyes off from Israel and put them on Jesus! Jesus is coming soon, Maranatha! He is ready to split the clouds of glory, be ready! Behold Him! Lift Him up! He said, "If I be lifted up," "*I*"—Jesus—not Israel or the Jewish people. I, too, say, "Lift Him up!"

If, no matter how evil it is now or may become, the worldly Israel is God's chosen forever, then Jesus' death on the Cross is meaningless. The only way then for the Gentiles to make Heaven their home is to be circumcised and become a Jew! Would that leave a female Gentile completely out, with no hope? Oh! I see! She cannot possibly be God's chosen!

I am not anti-Semitic or semi-Semitic, nor am I pro-Semitic. I love all races and all peoples. When Scripture tells us that there is no respect of persons with God, this means that He doesn't show any preference based on one's color, race, or national origin. I certainly want to be with God; therefore, I, too, must not show any partiality between one person and another.

Ezekiel 3:18 says that if we show partiality, respect or inequality, we have become workers of iniquity. And Jesus, in Matthew 7:23, said, ". . . I never knew you: depart from Me; ye that work iniquity."

Consequently, I must speak out against any teaching that God has a chosen race or nation. Matthew 28:18 tells us that God has turned all power in Heaven and earth over to Jesus. And Jesus, in John 3:16, said that, ". . . whosoever believeth in Him should not perish, but have everlasting life."

CHAPTER SEVEN

THE LAND PROMISE TO ISRAEL

> **Genesis 17:8**—And I will give unto thee, and to thy seed after thee, the land wherein thou art a stranger, all the land of Canaan, for an everlasting possession; and I will be their God.

God's promise of the land was everlasting but contains a condition that makes the actual possession of the land temporal. *What exactly was that condition?* That God would be their God! Everlasting means what it says. Not temporal, here today and gone tomorrow, but everlasting, forever. There has to be a reason then why the covenant was not everlasting. *Why was the covenant broken, with Israel losing their land? Why was Israel displaced and scattered throughout the world for over 2500 years? Why?* Because the land covenant could only last as long as the God-nation covenant remained unbroken.

Today, if we break our God-man relation, we lose our Jehovah-Jireh promise. God, if we choose to backslide, cannot keep us saved. And, likewise, God could not keep the Israelite nation whole, if they no longer chose to have Him as their God. This would go against a righteous God, and make Him unrighteous. The world would say, "Boy, the Jewish people can get away with anything! Why does God allow them to sin and not us?"

> **Deuteronomy 4:1 and 5:1-3**—Now therefore hearken, O Israel, unto the statutes and unto the judgments, which I teach you, for to do *them*, that ye may live, and go in and possess the land which the Lord God of your fathers giveth you . . . And Moses called all Israel, and said unto them, Hear O Israel, the statutes and judgments which I speak in your ears this day, that ye may learn them, and keep and do them. The Lord our God made a covenant with us in Horeb. The Lord made not this covenant with our fathers, but with us, *even* us, who *are* all of us here alive this day.

The land covenant would last only as long as Israel *observed God's statutes and kept His laws*. It replaced God's covenant with Abraham and wasn't inherited from Abraham or the fathers, but with the Israelite nation.

Israel had to keep their part of the covenant, or God would not be their God. If they broke the covenant, they would lose the land. Therefore, the land covenant becomes conditional and temporal, not everlasting. The Jewish people were dispersed and scattered to the four winds because the everlasting land promise was contingent upon Israel's obedience to God.

History confirms that the covenant was broken by Israel. Ever since Israel fell into the hands of Babylonia and its ruler, Nebuchadnezzar, it has never completely regained the entire promised land from the Tigris to the Euphrates River. Even today, Israel still possesses only about 5% of what was promised to them. If, in the past, Israel has completely lost all their land, how then can we say that the possession is an everlasting possession?

Was God unable to keep His part of the covenant? Was God inferior? No way! The Israelites lost their land because they allowed sin to separate them from God to the point where He was no longer their God. Even Daniel, Hananiah, Mishael, and Azariah were taken into slavery because of a disobedient nation. But praise God, He has always had a few, a remnant, a remaining seed that has chosen to serve Him.

Time after time the nation of Israel, because of their sin, has been cut off from God and sold into slavery. Today, because of sin, we sell ourselves into slavery to the Devil.

> **Genesis 17:8**—And I will give unto thee and to thy seed after thee, the land wherein thou art a stranger, all the land of Canaan, for a everlasting possession; And I will be their God.

This promise is a two part promise. First, the land of Canaan was to be an everlasting possession. *But it was not!* If the descendants of Abraham obeyed God and kept their part of the covenant, would they keep the land? Yes! Why then did Israel lose it? Why did they lose possession without a condition? The answer is simple—because there was a condition! It was there in the second part—"And I will be their God." A mere statement? A one way promise that God, unconditionally, without fail, would be their God even if they disobeyed and broke the covenant? Let's look more closely. God said, "I will be their God." But each of us is a free moral agent and, if we choose to do so, can allow any idol to become our god. Time after time God's people, the Israelites, broke the covenant that God would be their God by giving themselves over to other gods. This promise, then, is more of a covenant condition than it is a promise. It would be impossible for God to be their God if they worshiped Baal, a golden calf, or any other graven image. Therefore, if God is no longer their God, then the land is no longer theirs either and they cannot possess it.

The promises to Abraham's seed are narrowed to the descendants of Isaac, then to the descendants of Jacob, and finally, to the born-again in Christ, a descendant of David who, in turn, came from the linage of Abraham. The Abrahamic covenant is concluded in that it was conditional. God's promises have always been in conjunction with man's obedience.

John 4:22 tells us that, ". . . salvation is of the Jews." The first church was started by 12 apostles who were Jews. They were God's people, that is, they worshiped God and not an idol made with hands, or a false god, as Islam or Baal.

The commandments of the law were too numerous to mention; however, history will bear witness that all the commandments were broken. Time after time, the covenant was broken by Israel and reestablished by God.

> **Deuteronomy 30:16-20**—In that I command thee this day to love the Lord thy God, to walk in His ways, and to keep His commandments and His statutes, and His judgments, that thou mayest live and multiply: and the Lord thy God shall bless thee in the land whither thou goest to possess it. But if thine heart turn away, so that thou wilt not hear, but shalt be drawn away, and worship other gods, and serve them; I denounce unto you this day, that ye shall surely perish, *and that* ye shall not prolong *your* days,

upon the land, whither thou passest over Jordan to go to possess it. I call Heaven and earth to record this day against you, *that* I have set before you life and death, blessing and cursing: therefore choose life that both thou and thy seed may live: That thou mayest love the Lord thy God, *and* that thou mayest cleave unto Him: for He is thy life, and the length of thy days: that thou mayest dwell in the land which the Lord sware unto thy fathers, to Abraham, to Isaac, and to Jacob, to give them.

God said *if* they would obey His voice, they would dwell in the land. A blessing, or a curse? A blessing *if* they obeyed; a curse *if* they turned away and worshiped other gods. And, *if* they broke the covenant and turned away, they would lose the land.

Jeremiah 11:6-11—Then the Lord said unto me, Proclaim all these words in the cities of Judah, and in the streets of Jerusalem, saying, Hear ye the words of this covenant, and do them. For I earnestly protested unto your fathers in the day *that* I brought them up out of the land of Egypt, *even* unto this day, rising early and protesting, saying, Obey My voice. Yet they obeyed not, nor inclined their ear, but walked every one in the imagination of their evil heart: Therefore I will bring upon them all the words of this covenant, which I commanded *them* to do: but they did *them* not. And the Lord said unto me, A conspiracy is found among the men of Judah, and

among the inhabitants of Jerusalem. They
are turned back to the iniquities of their
forefathers, which refused to hear My
words; and they went after other gods to
serve them: the house of Israel and the
house of Judah have broken My covenant
which I made with their fathers. Therefore
thus saith the Lord, Behold, I will bring evil
upon them, which they shall not be able to
escape; and though they shall cry unto Me,
I will not hearken unto them.

God said that the Israelites, whom He brought up out of
the land of Egypt, obeyed not. The house of Israel and the
house of Judah broke the covenant and God would not hearken unto their cries.

Deuteronomy 28:15, 25—But it shall
come to pass, if thou wilt not hearken unto
the voice of the Lord thy God, to observe
to do all His commandments and His statutes which I command thee this day; that
all these curses shall come upon thee, and
overtake thee . . . The Lord shall cause thee
to be smitten before thine enemies, thou
shalt go out one way against them, and flee
seven ways before them: and shalt be removed into all the kingdoms of the earth.

If Israel would obey and keep all of God's commandments, He would bless them in the promised land; however,
if they failed to obey, He would smite them and cause them to
be scattered into all the kingdoms of the earth. This has been
fulfilled! God's land promise will be fulfilled in Christ!

63

CHAPTER EIGHT

THE PROMISES TO ABRAHAM

> **Genesis 12:1-2**—Now the Lord had said
> unto Abram, Get thee out of thy country,
> and from thy kindred, and from thy father's
> house, unto a land that I will shew thee:
> And I will make of thee a great nation, and
> I will bless thee, and make thy name great;
> and thou shalt be a blessing:

God's promise to Abram was that He would show him a
land and make of him a great nation.

> **Genesis 12:5, 7**—. . . into the land of
> Canaan they came . . . And the Lord ap-
> peared unto Abram, and said, Unto thy seed
> will I give this land . . .

These promises were fulfilled; God did show Abram the
promised land.   Abram left and journeyed to Egypt, where
he was expelled. Upon his return to Bethel, God renewed the
promise of the land.

Genesis 17:7-9—And I will establish My covenant between Me and thee and thy seed after thee in their generations for an everlasting covenant, to be a God unto thee, and to thy seed after thee. And I will give unto thee, and to thy seed after thee, the land wherein thou art a stranger, all the land of Canaan, for an everlasting possession; and I will be their God. And God said unto Abraham, Thou shalt keep My covenant therefore, thou, and thy seed after thee in their generations.

Psalm 105:8-11—He hath remembered His covenant for ever, the Word *which* He commanded to a thousand generations. Which *covenant* He made with Abraham, and His oath unto Isaac; and confirmed the same unto Jacob for a law, *and* to Israel for an everlasting covenant: Saying, Unto thee will I give the land of Canaan, the lot of your inheritance.

Psalms 105:45—That they might observe His statutes, and keep His laws . . .

The Covenant was to be renewed from generation to generation with Isaac, Jacob, and the Israelites. It was given to Abraham with the warning, "and I will be their God." This promise was renewed with Isaac because of God's promise to Abraham as stated in Genesis 26:3.

The land covenant God made with Israel would last only as long as Israel, "observed His statutes and kept His laws."

> **Galatians 3:16, 29, 27, 28**—Now to Abraham and his seed were the promises made . . . which is Christ . . . and if ye be Christ's, then are ye Abraham's seed, and heirs according to the promise . . . For ye are all the children of God by faith in Christ Jesus . . . For as many of you as have been baptized into Christ have put on Christ. There is neither Jew nor Greek, there is neither bond nor free, there is neither male nor female: for ye are all one in Christ Jesus.

We, then, are one in Christ Jesus and one with the Jews. We, too, have received all the blessings and promises ever made by God or Jesus, concerning His children and Jesus' brethren.

> **Galatians 3:14, 9**—That the blessing of Abraham might come on the Gentiles through Jesus Christ; that we might receive the promise of the Spirit through faith . . . So then they which be of faith are blessed with faithful Abraham.

Praise God! We, the Gentiles, are equal with our Jewish brethren! And, just as our Jewish brethren were punished for their sin, we Gentiles will also be punished if we fail to keep our sins under the Blood of Jesus.

Whether Jew or Gentile, God's blessings come to us only if we obey Him! Nationality means nothing! If we have not, as individuals, accepted Christ, we will not make Heaven our home. Again, I quote from Romans 2:11, "For there is no respect of person with God."

Saved by grace? Regardless of sin in one's life? Absolutely not! *Saved by nationality? Regardless of the sin?* God forbid! Absolutely not! It was because of his disobedience that Abraham never possessed the land that was promised.

Most of the promises God made to Abraham have been fulfilled. Let us look at those promises:

1. Abraham's name shall be great.

This has been fulfilled!

2. Abraham shall have great blessings.

> **This has been fulfilled!** Abraham and Lot had such great worldly possessions that their sheep and cattle herders strove amongst themselves. And, one cannot overlook the miracle of Issac's birth when Abraham was 99 years of age and his wife, Sarah, was 90!

3. Whoever blesses Abraham will be blessed; and whoever curses Abraham will be cursed.

> **This has been fulfilled!** We can see entire families today that are under the blessing or the curse, depending on how they treat God's people!

4. From Abraham will come a great nation.

This has been fulfilled!

5. Abraham will be the father of many nations.

This has been fulfilled!

6. Kings shall come from the line of Abraham.

This has been fulfilled! Fulfilled by Solomon, David, Saul, and others!

7. Abraham's seed shall inherit the land from the river of Egypt to the Euphrates River, as an everlasting possession.

Annulled and broken! To be set up again after the tribulation!

8. God will be the God of Abraham and his seed forever.

Broken! To be renewed for the duration of the Millennial Reign!

9. Abraham's seed shall conquer their enemies.

This has been fulfilled! Fulfilled on many occasions!

10. In Abraham's seed all nations of the earth shall be blessed.

This has been fulfilled! Fulfilled by Christ!

11. The covenant with Abraham shall be an everlasting covenant.

Annulled and broken! Abraham did not possess the land. This covenant, as stated in Hebrews 8:6-13 and Jeremiah 31:31, was changed to a new and better covenant. The old covenant has been done away with. In Hebrews 8:13, Paul said it "decayeth." They no longer possess the ark which is the crux of their covenant. The ark had the golden pot which contained manna from Mose's day, Aaron's rod that budded. It also contained the tables of the law. The law which is done away with in Christ. If the law is reestablished—then Christ is done away with. And, Heaven forbid, that can never be! Hebrews 8:7 tells us that if that first covenant had been faultless, then no place should have been sought for the second!

CHAPTER NINE

GOD'S PROMISES TO DAVID

Abraham's promises from God were renewed with Isaac, Jacob, then with Israel and David.

> **II Samuel 7:10-16**—Moreover I will appoint a place for My people Israel, and will plant them, that they may dwell in a place of their own, and move no more; neither shall the children of wickedness afflict them any more, as before time, And as since the time that I commanded judges *to be over* My people Israel, and have caused thee to rest from all thine enemies. Also the Lord telleth thee that He will make thee an house. and when thy days be fulfilled, and thou shalt sleep with thy fathers, I will set up thy seed after thee, which shall proceed out of thy bowels, and I will establish His Kingdom. He shall build an house for My name, and I will establish the Throne of his King-

> dom forever. I will be his Father, and he shall be My Son, If He commit iniquity, I will chasten Him with the rod of men, and with the stripes of the children of men: But My mercy shall not depart away from Him, as I took *it* from Saul, whom I put away before thee. And thine house and thy kingdom shall be established for ever before thee: thy throne shall be established for ever.

God promised David that Israel would dwell in a place of their own and move no more. He also promised that He would raise up One to sit on David's throne, and His Throne would be established forever. According to Luke 1:32, 33 and Acts 2:30 this was fulfilled by Jesus.

> **Acts 13:23**—Of this man's seed hath God according to *His* promise raised unto Israel a Savior, Jesus.

> **Luke 24:47**—And that repentance and remission of sins should be preached in His name among all nations, beginning at Jerusalem.

Yes, both the Jews and the Gentiles have to repent! Or, as Romans 9:14 puts it, "What shall we say then? Is there unrighteousness with God? God forbid!" I join Paul in saying, "God forbid!" God is not an unrighteous God. If we separate the Jew from the Gentile and say that God will respect one and not the other, we have erred and become workers of iniquity. Man may see and make a difference between black and white, Jew and Gentile, Samaritan and Israelite; however, God does not. Every person must come to Him by way of Jesus and His Cross. If not, the Cross means nothing and Jesus died in vain.

If we must separate race from race in order to prove a doctrinal point, then that doctrinal point could very well be wrong. It is better that we choose a more spiritual route and not err from the truth in God.

When Israel is restored in all of her glory, possessing the entire promised land, will God restore the mercy seat, the ark of testimony, and the temple in Jerusalem? *Will such a restoration cause the Israelites to accept Christ as their Messiah?* These questions, and more, arise as we study. Again, will such a restoration cause the Jewish people to turn to Christ? Think about it! God has restored many things to them: wealth, health, and power. And, he has done so without Christ. *Do we really expect this overwhelming shower of blessings to do for them what the Cross could not?*

Man is still seeking great wealth and land possessions. Jesus said, "Lay ye up treasures in Heaven." A man, in Luke 12:18, 20, 21 said, ". . . I will pull down my barns and build greater . . ." The Lord answered, "Thou fool, this night thy soul shall be required of thee . . . So is he that layeth up treasure for himself, and is not rich toward God."

72

CHAPTER TEN

GOD'S PROMISE TO SOLOMON

I Kings 9:4-9—And if thou wilt walk before Me, as David thy father walked, in integrity of heart, and in uprightness, to do according to all that I have commanded thee, *and* wilt keep My statutes and My judgments: Then I will establish the throne of thy kingdom upon Israel for ever, as I promised to David thy father, saying, There shall not fail thee a man upon the throne of Israel. *But* if ye shall at all turn from following Me, ye or your children, and will not keep My commandments *and* My statutes which I have set before you, but go and serve other gods, and worship them: then will I cut off Israel out of the land which I have given them; and this house, which I have hallowed for My name, will I cast out of My sight; and Israel shall be a proverb and a byword among all people: And at this house, *which* is high, every one that passeth by it shall be astonished, and shall hiss; and they shall say, Why hath the Lord done thus unto this land, and to this house? And they shall answer, Because they forsook the Lord their God, who brought forth their fathers out of the land of Egypt, and have taken hold upon other gods, and have worshiped them, and served them: therefore hath the Lord brought upon them all this evil.

God promised Solomon that as long as they kept His statutes and judgments, the Temple and land would belong to Israel; however, *if* they were to serve other gods, He would cut them out of the land which He had given them. This covenant promise and condition replaced the Davidic covenant which, in turn, replaced the covenant made with Abraham.

Why did God allow Israel to be scattered and lose their land? Why was the temple destroyed? Why is David's throne unoccupied today? Because they forsook the Lord as their God and broke the everlasting land covenant He made with them.

The old covenant has been broken and is no longer in effect. It has been replaced by an everlasting covenant—a covenant in Christ! If the old covenant, the land covenant had not been broken, Solomon's temple would still be standing, and a descendent of David would still be sitting on his throne.

The covenant God made with Abraham, Isaac, Jacob, David, and Solomon, although made to individuals, affected the entire nation. Today, we should thank God that He, through the New covenant made in Jesus, deals not with nations, but with individuals! The promise God made in the old covenant will be reestablished, reaffirmed, and fulfilled in Jesus Christ.

CHAPTER ELEVEN

THE PROMISE OF A NEW NAME

Isaiah 65:1-3, 8-15—I am sought of *them that* asked not *for Me*; I am found of *them that* sought Me not; I said, Behold Me, behold Me, unto a nation *that* was not called by My name. I have spread out My hands all the day unto a rebellious people, which walketh in a way *that was* not good, after their own thoughts; A people that provoketh Me to anger continually to My face; that sacrificeth in gardens, and burneth incense upon altars of brick . . . Thus saith the Lord, As the new wine is found in the cluster, and one saith, Destroy it not; for a blessing *is* in it: so will I do for My servants' sakes, that I may not destroy them all. And I will bring forth a seed out of Jacob, and out of Judah an inheritor of My mountains: and Mine elect shall inherit it, and My servants shall dwell there. And Sharon shall be a fold of flocks, and the valley of Achor a place for the herds to lie down in, for My people that have sought Me. But ye *are* they that forsake the Lord, that forget My holy mountain, that prepare a table for that troop, and that furnish the drink offering unto that number. Therefore will I number you to the sword, and ye shall all bow down to the slaughter: because when I called, ye did not answer; when I spake, ye did not hear: but did evil before Mine eyes, and did choose *that* wherein I delighted not. Therefore thus saith the Lord God, Behold, My servants shall eat, but ye shall be hungry: behold, My servants shall drink, but ye shall be thirsty: Behold, My servants shall rejoice, but ye shall be ashamed: Behold My servants shall sing for joy of heart, but ye shall cry for sorrow of heart, and shall howl for vexation of spirit. And ye shall leave your name for a curse unto My chosen: for the Lord God shall slay thee, and call His servants by another name:

God said that Israel was rebellious and had provoked Him to anger; however, He would not destroy them all. He said He would leave a remnant that He would call "servants" and "elect" and that this remnant would inherit the mountains and dwell there. God will bring forth a seed out of Jacob but, according to these Scriptures, Israel, on the whole, will forsake Him. God will leave their name for a curse unto His chosen and they will be slain. They will not enter the Millennial Kingdom; instead, God will call His servants— the elect, chosen, children of Israel, brethren, remnant, seed, heirs—by another name. Could that name be *Christian*?

Romans 10:20-21—But Esaias is very bold, and saith, I was found of them that sought Me not; I was made manifest unto them that asked not after Me. But to Israel He saith, All day long I have stretched forth My hands unto a disobedient and gainsaying people.

Paul is quoting Isaiah and bringing the interpretation up to date. Again, the people of Israel, on the whole, are a disobedient people.

Romans 11:5, 7, 23—Even so then at this present time also there is a remnant according to the election of grace. What then? Israel hath not obtained that which He seeketh for; but the election hath obtained it, and the rest were blinded . . . And they also, if they abide not still in unbelief, shall be graffed in: for God is able to graff them in again.

God still has a remnant, the election of grace, those which have been saved in Jesus' blood. Saved, not because of the Israelite covenant, but saved as it says in Hebrews 10:20, "by the new and living way." That new and living way is Jesus! Those who abide in their belief in Jesus are saved because they are graffed in again.

CHAPTER TWELVE

THE PROMISE OF THE REGATHERING

Mark 13:20-27—And except that the Lord had shortened those days, no flesh should be saved: but for the elect's sake, whom He hath chosen, He hath shortened the days. And then if any man shall say to you, Lo, here *is* Christ; or, lo, *He is* there; believe *him* not: For false Christs and false prophets shall rise, and shall shew signs and wonders, to seduce, if *it were* possible, even the elect. But take ye heed: behold, I have foretold you all things. But in those days, after that tribulation, the sun shall be darkened, and the moon shall not give her light. And the stars of Heaven shall fall, and the powers that are in Heaven shall be shaken. And then shall they see the Son of Man coming in the clouds with great power and glory. And then shall He send His angels and shall gather together His elect from the four winds, from the uttermost part of the earth to the uttermost part of Heaven.

It is clear that the gathering of the elect at the end of time is not a regathering of Jews, in particular, but a gathering of the elect. The elect will be gathered out of Heaven and out of the earth, those that have preceded the rapture, those that have gone in the rapture and those that are saved during the tribulation.

> **Isaiah 11:1, 4, 6-12**—And there shall come forth a rod out of the stem of Jesse, and a Branch shall grow out of his roots . . . But with righteousness shall He judge the poor, and reprove with equity for the meek of the earth: and He shall smite the earth with the rod of His mouth, and with the breath of His lips shall He slay the wicked . . . The wolf also shall dwell with the lamb, and the leopard shall lie down with the kid; and the calf and the young lion and the fatling together; and a little child shall lead them. And the cow and the bear shall feed; their young ones shall lie down together: and the lion shall eat straw like the ox. And the sucking child shall play on the hole of the asp, and the weaned child shall put his hand on the cockatrice' den. They shall not hurt nor destroy in all My holy mountain: for the earth shall be full of the knowledge of the Lord, as the waters cover the sea. And in that day there shall be a root of Jesse, which shall stand for an ensign of the people; to it shall the Gentiles seek: and His rest shall be glorious. And it shall come to pass in that day, *that* the Lord shall set His hand again the second time to recover the remnant of His people, which shall be

> left, from Assyria, and from Egypt, and
> from Pathros, and from Cush, and from
> Elam, and from Shinar, and from Hamath,
> and from the islands of the sea. And he
> shall set up an ensign for the nations, and
> shall assemble the outcasts of Israel, and
> gather together the dispersed of Judah from
> the four corners of the earth.

The Stem of Jesse is, of course, Jesus Christ. The government will be upon His shoulders. The time of gathering together is not to take place until during the Millennial Reign.

> **Ezekiel 37:12**—Therefore prophesy and
> say unto them, Thus saith the Lord God;
> Behold O My people, I will open your
> graves, and cause you to come up out of
> your graves, and bring you into the land of
> Israel.

The time is after the rapture, after the resurrection, during the Millenium. A time when the animals will be vegetarians, at peace, and not prey on one another. Ezekiel 38:11 says Israel will be at peace and Jerusalem will be without walls. Except for a brief period during David's reign, as described in Second Samuel 7:11, at no time in the 2500 year history of Israel have they been at peace and able to dwell without walls. Even today, Israel is trying to overrun the Palestine Arabs and drive them from the land.

Matthew 24:6 tells us that until the rapture there will be no peace, only wars and rumors of wars. Therefore, the regathering spoken of in Isaiah 11:10-12 and in Ezekiel 37:12 will have to be after the first resurrection.

The Gentile shall seek the Lord, the root of Jesse. The remnant to be recovered are the outcast of Israel and the dispersed of Judah that were scattered to the four corners of the earth. Note that only a remnant is to be saved and regathered—the believers in the Stem of Jesse, the Branch, Jesus Christ. Daniel 12 and Revelation 16 tells us that all the others either were not resurrected during the first resurrection or were destroyed during the Holocaust, the seven years of tribulation.

Many look at modern day Israel and their restoration as a nation to be the sign that the Lord is coming soon. However, the "sign" of the Israelites returning to their homeland does not necessarily have any bearing on the promise of the regathering. The regathering will be a gathering of the elect as individuals and not the gathering of Israel as a nation.

If Israel wishes to dwell in the homeland during the Millennium, they will have to enter by way of The Door, Jesus Christ. The "election of grace" in Romans 11:5-7 are the only ones to be "regathered." They are the "remnant" Isaiah 11:11 speaks of and the ones who were found "written in the Book" as described in Daniel 12:1.

CHAPTER THIRTEEN

GOD BROKE HIS PROMISE

Amos 4:6, 7, 9-12—And I also have given you . . . want of bread . . . I have withholden the rain . . . I have smitten you with blasting and mildew . . . the palmerworm devoured . . . I have sent among you pestilence . . . your young men have I slain with the sword . . . I have overthrown *some* of you . . . yet have ye not returned unto Me, saith the Lord. Therefore thus will I do unto thee, O Israel: and because I will do this unto thee, prepare to meet thy God, O Israel.

Amos 5:11, 17—Forasmuch therefore as your treading *is* upon the poor, and ye take from him burdens of wheat: ye have built houses of hewn stone, but ye shall not dwell in them; ye have planted pleasant vineyards, but ye shall not drink wine of them . . . *And* in all vineyards *shall* be wailing: for I will pass through thee, saith the Lord.

> **Amos 9:9-10**—For lo, I will command, and
> I will sift the house of Israel among all na-
> tions, like as *corn* is sifted in a sieve, yet
> shall not the least grain fall upon the earth.
> All the sinners of My people shall die by
> the sword . . .

God sent famine, pestilence, drought and war, to get Israel to return to Him and they would not. Today, God is still
trying to get Israel to see their need of a Savior and come to
Him by way of The Door—Jesus Christ.

I once spoke with a Jewish woman, who during World
War II, had been a prisoner in a German concentration camp.
All around her was death. She witnessed the slaughter of
one-third of the then known Jewish population. This woman
told me that she sometimes wished that she wasn't one of
God's chosen—that God deals too harshly with His people.

*In times past, why were the Israelites cut off and scat-
tered from their land to the four winds?* Because they disobeyed God by serving other gods and denied Jesus as their
Messiah.

> **Judges 2:1-2**—And an angel of the Lord
> came up from Gilgal to Bochim, and said,
> I made you to go up out of Egypt, and have
> brought you unto the land which I sware
> unto your fathers; and I said, I will never
> break My covenant with you. And ye shall
> make no league with the inhabitants of this
> land; ye shall throw down their altars: but
> ye have not obeyed My voice: why have
> ye done this?

God promised not to break His covenant with Israel. But
then He asked, "Why have *you* broken My covenant?"

Numbers 14:34—After the number of the days in which ye searched the land, *even* forty days, each day for a year, shall ye bear your iniquities, *even* forty years, and ye shall know My breach of promise.

God said, "and ye shall know My breach of promise." To *breach* a promise is to *break* it.

Zechariah 11:10-13—And I took My staff, *even* Beauty, and cut it asunder, that I might break My covenant which I had made with all the people. And it was broken in that day: and so the poor of the flock that waited upon Me knew that it *was* the Word of the Lord. And I said unto them, if ye think good, give *Me* My price; and if not, forbear. So they weighed for My price thirty *pieces* of silver. And the Lord said unto me, Cast it unto the potter: a goodly price that I was prised at of them. And I took the thirty *pieces* of silver, and cast them to the potter in the House of the Lord.

Matthew 26 and 27 says there was a man—Jesus of Galilee—who was sold for thirty pieces of silver. The thirty pieces of silver were cast down in the temple at the feet of the chief priest and elders. Later, the chief priest took those same thirty pieces of silver and used it to buy the potter's field.

Zechariah 12:10 and 13:1—And I will pour upon the house of David, and upon the inhabitants of Jerusalem, the spirit of grace and of supplications: and they shall look upon Me whom they have pierced, and

84

> they shall mourn for Him as one mourneth
> for *His* only *Son*, and shall be in bitterness
> for Him, as one that is in bitterness for *His*
> first born . . . In that day there shall be a
> fountain opened to the house of David and
> to the inhabitants of Jerusalem for sin and
> for uncleanness.

Jesus, the only begotten Son of God was pierced, opening the fountain for forgiveness of sin to the house of David. Jesus' body was broken! Those who waited on the Lord looking for the Messiah knew that He was the fulfillment of the prophecy. God, through Jesus, *broke the covenant* with the people.

Jesus was the Staff of Beauty. The Staff was broken on that day. So also was the covenant with the nation of Israel. Jesus is now the covenant, it is no longer with a nation, but with any individual from any nation who will come to Him.

Yes, God broke His promise to the children of Israel, *but* only after they broke their covenant with Him.

> **Amos 8:2**—And He said, Amos, what seest
> thou? And I said, A basket of summer fruit.
> Then said the Lord unto me, The end is
> come upon My people of Israel and with
> the house of Judah . . .

In Genesis 6:3, God said that His Spirit would not always strive with man. The covenant was broken by Israel time after time, but now there is a new covenant—a covenant with the elect.

> **Romans 11:7**—What then? Israel hath not
> obtained that which he seeketh for; but the
> election hath obtained it . . .

Exodus 32:33—And the Lord said unto Moses, Whosoever hath sinned against Me, him will I blot out of My book.

Psalms 89:3-4—I have made a covenant with My chosen, I have sworn unto David My servant, Thy seed will I establish for ever, and build up thy throne to all generations.

God swore unto David his seed would sit on his throne to all generations. This can only be Jesus on the throne of David during the Millennium when all generations are present.

Romans 11:26—And so all Israel shall be saved: as it is written, There shall come out of Sion the Deliverer, and shall turn away ungodliness from Jacob:

So, all of Israel that go into the Millennium shall be saved!

Ezekiel 20:34-38—And I will bring you out from the people, and will gather you out of the countries wherein ye are scattered, with a mighty hand, and with a stretched out arm, and with fury poured out. And I will bring you into the wilderness of the people, and there will I plead with you face to face. Like as I pleaded with your fathers in the wilderness of the land of Egypt, so will I plead with you, saith the Lord God. And I will cause you to pass under the rod, and I will bring you into the bond of the covenant: And I will purge out from among you the rebels, and them that transgress against Me:

86

> I will bring them forth out of the country
> where they sojourn, and they shall not en-
> ter into the land of Israel: and ye shall know
> that I *am* the Lord.

Israel will be gathered out of the countries where they are scattered and the sheep of Israel will be separated from the goats of Israel. This is another way of saying that the rebels will be purged. The goats, rebels, and transgressors will not enter into the Millennial land of Israel!

> **Jeremiah 3:14-16**—Turn, O backsliding
> children, saith the Lord; for I am married
> unto you: and I will take you one of a city,
> and two of a family, and I will bring you to
> Zion: And I will give you pastors accord-
> ing to Mine heart, which shall feed you with
> knowledge and understanding. And it shall
> come to pass, when ye be multiplied and
> increased in the land, in those days, saith
> the Lord, they shall say no more, The ark
> of the covenant of the Lord: neither shall
> it come to mind: neither shall they remem-
> ber it: neither shall they visit *it*: neither
> shall *that* be done any more.

God declares that He will bring them "one of a city, and two of a family," and bring them to Zion! The Ark of the Covenant shall be with Israel no more. I ask, *"Where is the Ark today?"* Many men of renown have searched the world over for this Ark, without which the temple will be a hollow mockery with *Ichabod*—"God hath departed"—written on the door. Man continues to look for the Ark. God laughs at their foolishness, for they shall not find it anywhere on earth. One individual has spent his entire life in the search. He thinks he has found it and is now trying to persuade others that the Ark is to be found in a monastery high in the mountains of Ethiopia. Another man thinks he has found the Ark behind a huge rock in the wall of Jerusalem.

Some believe that Israel will rebuild the temple on the holy grounds of Jerusalem during the tribulation. In my opinion, this belief is in direct disobedience and an abomination to God. Jesus is the Temple! He has replaced God's law covenant with Israel, if only they will accept. If rebuilt, the temple will be incomplete because it will not have the Ark, wherein rest the Ten Commandments, the manna from the wilderness, and Aaron's rod.

Where is the Ark? It is recorded in the Book: scripture and verse. So let them look, search, and guess. If God permits, I will give the complete answer to this question in another book. Until that day, if anyone writes for the answer, the precise passage of Scripture will be given.

Israel makes a treaty with Hell; another abomination unto God.

> **Isaiah 28:15-18**—Because ye have said, We have made a covenant with death, and with Hell are we at agreement; when the overflowing scourge shall pass through, it shall not come unto us: for we have made lies our refuge, and under falsehood have we hid ourselves: Therefore thus saith the Lord God, Behold, I lay in Zion for a foundation a stone, a tried stone, a precious corner *stone*, a sure foundation: he that believeth shall not make haste. Judgment also will I lay to the line, and righteousness to the plummet: and the hail shall sweep away the refuge of lies, and the waters shall

overflow the hiding place. And your covenant with death shall be disannuled, and
your agreement with Hell shall not stand;
when the overflowing scourge shall pass
through, then ye shall be trodden down by
it.

Their treaty with Hell shall not stand and, unless they
come back to God, Israel will be destroyed. There is no way
that God can bless them if they are in cohorts with the Devil;
nor can He be their God.

Matthew 21:33-43—Hear another parable:
There was a certain householder, which
planted a vineyard, and hedged it round
about, and digged a winepress in it, and
built a tower, and let it out to husbandmen,
and went into a far country: And when the
time of the fruit drew near, he sent his servants to the husbandmen, that they might
receive the fruits of it. And the husbandmen took his servants, and beat one, and
killed another, and stoned another. Again,
he sent other servants more than the first:
and they did unto them likewise. But last
of all he sent unto them his son, saying,
They will reverence my son. But when the
husbandmen saw the son, they said among
themselves, This is the heir: come, let us
kill him, and let us seize on his inheritance.
And they caught him, and cast *him* out of
the vineyard, and slew *him*. When the lord
therefore of the vineyard cometh, what will
he do unto those husbandmen? They say
unto him, He will miserably destroy those

wicked men, and will let out of *his* vineyard unto other husbandmen, which shall
render him the fruits in their seasons. Jesus
saith unto them, Did ye never read in the
Scriptures, The stone which the builders
rejected, the same is become the head of
the corner: this is the Lord's doing, and it
is marvellous in our eyes? Therefore say I
unto you, The Kingdom of God shall be
taken from you, and given to a nation bringing forth the fruits thereof.

In this parable God is the householder; Israel is the vineyard, the rulers of Israel are the husbandmen; and the servants are Moses, the prophets, and the twelve apostles. The
Son, of course, is Jesus.

God sent Moses, the prophets, John the Baptist, Paul,
and the apostles to Israel, His vineyard. Some were beaten
and some were killed. He then sent His Son, Jesus, and they
would not hear Him. Instead, they killed the heir and took
the inheritance. *What did God say He would do with the
rebels of Israel?* He said that He would take the Kingdom of
God from them and give it to a nation that serves Him! That
nation will be the New Jerusalem of the Millennial Reign!
But can Israel return? Yes, the sheep can, but not the goats.

Romans 11:23—And they also, if they
abide not still in unbelief, shall be graffed
in: for God is able to graff them in again.

*How many of those who have returned to Israel have
really returned to God? Did they just return to the land and
not to God—only to lose it all at the last trump?*
I once heard a man give his testimony in which he ex-
pressed his desire to become a Jew so that he could become

one of God's chosen people. Later, he searched out a Jewish woman, married her, and converted to Judaism. He did so, mistakenly believing that if he returned to Israel with his bride that they would be there when God ushered in His Kingdom.

What causes people to believe and give credence to such false teachings? At best, this man and his wife will go through the tribulation. There, he will find that for them to enter into the Kingdom of God, they will have to be counted as sheep and not as goats. And, according to John 3:5, for one to enter the Kingdom of God and be counted as a sheep, he must be born again in Jesus.

Return to the land? Yes, they, the Jewish people will return to the land, if for no other reason than to fulfill the prophecy that they would! *Return to Israel!* Good! Return, if you must; *but*, first accept Jesus as the Messiah! Then, return as a missionary for Him!

CHAPTER FOURTEEN

GOD'S ETERNAL PROMISE

Come to the God of promise and not the land! Come to the new covenant!

> **Jeremiah 31:31-33 and Hebrews 8:8-10**—Behold, the days come, saith the Lord, that I will make a new covenant with the house of Israel and with the house of Judah. Not according to the covenant that I made with their fathers in the day *that* I took them by the hand to bring them out of the land of Egypt; which My covenant they brake, although I was an husband unto them, saith the Lord: But this *shall* be the covenant that I will make with the house of Israel; After those days, saith the Lord, I will put My law in their inward parts, and write it in their hearts; and will be their God, and they shall be My people.

A new covenant! Not according to the covenant of Abraham, Isaac, Jacob and Israel, but a new covenant! Israel broke the old covenant leaving God no choice but to do away with it and replace it with a new one. This new covenant is Christ:

> **Hebrews 9:11-12**—But Christ being come an high priest of good things to come, by a greater and more perfect tabernacle, not made with hands, that is to say, not of this building; Neither by the blood of goats and calves, but by His own Blood He entered in once into the holy place, having obtained eternal redemption *for us*.

When Paul said, "eternal redemption *for us*," he was speaking of Israel and the everlasting promise God made to the Jewish people. Now, if the new and everlasting covenant can only be obtained through Christ, how can some still claim that it comes by being a descendant of Abraham? The promise God made to Abraham is fulfilled in Christ! It is He who will fulfill the everlasting covenant and sit on the throne of David.

> **Hebrews 10:16-21**—This *is* the covenant that I will make with them after those days, saith the Lord, I will put My laws into their hearts, and in their minds will I write them; And their sins and iniquities will I remember no more. Now where remission of these *is, there is* no more offering for sin. Having therefore, brethren, boldness to enter into the holiest by the Blood of Jesus, By a new and living way, which He hath consecrated for us, through the veil, that is to say, His flesh; And *having* an High Priest over the house of God.

Yes, the new covenant is Jesus—the new and living way that Jeremiah prophesied about. Those who have Jesus are the people of God! The chosen ones! "And I will be their God and they shall be My people."

Israel's sins will be removed by God only because they have been purchased by Jesus' Blood. All the sacrifices and oblations of the old order as an offering for sin have been done away with—replaced by Christ! No longer is there a need to offer the blood of bulls and goats. To continue with the old and not accept the new would be an abomination to God and would mean that Jesus died in vain.

> **John 1:11-13**—He came unto His own, and His own received Him not. But as many as received Him, to them gave He power to become the sons of God, *even* to them that believe on His name: Which were born, not of blood, nor of the will of the flesh, nor of the will of man, but of God.

"He came unto His own." *Why were the Jewish people and nation, "His own?"* Because they were the only ones who would know Him. All others were heathen nations and would not recognize Him. He had to come to the only nation and people who had been taught the Word and not to a nation that would worship Dagon, the god of the sun, or some other pagan god. That is why He chose Israel and why the Israelites have always been His Chosen people.

His own, on the whole, received Him not, but as many as did receive Him and believe on His name, became the sons of God. These were not born through the natural will of the flesh or the blood line of Abraham, Isaac, Jacob, Judah, or David, they were *born again*! Born again of God! Born again spiritual! The source? The spiritual seed of their rebirth?—Jesus!!!

94

CHAPTER FIFTEEN

ONE MORE PROMISE

II chronicles 7:14—If My people, which
are called by My name, shall humble themselves, and pray, and seek My face, and turn
from their wicked ways; then will I hear
from Heaven, and will forgive their sin, and
will heal their land.

God has given us this promise. A promise that will stand
for all generations. Israel can return, "one in a city and two of
a family," but only in Jesus Christ! In other words, they can
return only as individuals by way of the Cross and not as a
nation. Jesus, in John 10:9, 1, said, "I am the Door: by Me if
any man enter in, he shall be saved . . . he that entereth not by
the Door . . . the same is a thief and a robber."

When Jesus said, "It is finished," and died on the Cross,
God broke or replaced the law covenant with Israel. In Matthew 5:17, Jesus said, "Think not that I am come to destroy
the law or the prophets: I am not come to destroy, but to
fulfill."

> **Isaiah 7:14**—Therefore the Lord Himself
> shall give you a sign; Behold a virgin shall
> conceive, and bear a son, and shall call His
> name Immanuel.

Jesus is Immanuel! My dear Jewish friends, if you want to come back to God, you cannot reject Jesus! If you want to dwell in the holy land during the Millennium, you must first come to God through Jesus and not the law covenant or the land of Israel. Romans 11:23 assures you that if you abide not still in unbelief, you can be graffed in again.

Most, if not all, of the Jewish people believe in God, sacrifices, tithes, Abraham, Isaac, Jacob, Moses and the prophets. *What then is the unbelief that causes them to be broken off?* It is their unbelief that Jesus is the Messiah—their King and Savior. They are broken off because they don't believe in Jesus!

They stubbornly cling to the mistaken belief that just because they are Israelites and God made a covenant with Israel that they will get into His kingdom. They refuse to recognize that the covenant in which they place so much faith was done away with in Christ!

> **John 3:5**—Jesus answered, Verily, verily,
> I say unto thee, Except a man be born of
> water and *of* the Spirit, he cannot enter into
> the Kingdom of God.

Unless a man, including the Jew, is born again, he cannot enter the Kingdom of God! These words were written to all of us, not just the Jewish people. *Why?* As a reminder that we should take heed and not fall into the same example of unbelief.

CHAPTER SIXTEEN

GOD KEPT HIS PROMISE

God promised Israel:

That a son would be born of a virgin.

Isaiah 7:14—. . . Behold, a virgin shall conceive, and bear a son, and shall call His name Immanuel.

That He would take away their sins.

Jeremiah 31:34—. . . I will forgive their iniquity, and I will remember their sin no more.

God gave Israel a new covenant in Jesus and took away the sins of all who believed in Him.

Hebrews 10:16, 21—This *is* the covenant that I will make with them after those days, saith the Lord, I will put My laws into their

hearts, and in their minds will I write them
. . . And having an High Priest over the
house of God . . .

God has already given the new covenant to Israel—the
house of God—with Jesus being the High Priest. Whoever
will, may come! It is *my* choice! It is *your* choice! It is *our*
choice! And, it is *their* choice! Whoever will come, surely
means me! With God there is no respect of person!

> **Galatians 3:26-29**—For ye are all the chil-
> dren of God by faith in Christ Jesus, For as
> many of you as have been baptized into
> Christ have put on Christ. There is neither
> Jew nor Greek, there is neither bond nor
> free, there is neither male or female: for ye
> are all one in Christ Jesus. And if ye *be*
> Christ's, then are ye Abraham's seed, and
> heirs according to the promise.

Anyone can claim the promise!

> **Galatians 3:1-3**—O foolish Galatians, who
> hath bewitched you, that ye should not obey
> the truth, before whose eyes Jesus Christ
> hath been evidently set forth, crucified
> among you? This only would I learn of
> you, Received ye the Spirit by the works of
> the law, or by the hearing of faith? Are ye
> so foolish? having begun in the Spirit, are
> ye now made perfect by the flesh?

Oh foolish *Galatians*! Oh foolish *Israelites*! Oh foolish
Gentiles! Oh foolish *church members*! Oh foolish *Christians*! Who hath bewitched you?

We should strive to keep our eyes on Jesus and not the natural. In doing so, we remain spiritual! Anyone who does not believe and breaks the new covenant with God will lose the promise of Jesus! Let us take our eyes off from Israel and follow Christ—off from the flesh and onto the Spirit!

CHAPTER SEVENTEEN

THE JUDGMENT

In 1946 a man, based on his belief that a generation was set at 20 years, predicted that the end of time would occur in May of that year. Another man, a minister, made a similar prediction and convinced his family and entire congregation to leave California and go with him to Arkansas. On the chosen day the multitude, dressed in white, proceeded to the top of a hillside at high noon to wait for the Lord's return. They did these things in spite of Jesus' admonition:

> **Luke 17:20**—. . . The Kingdom of God cometh not with observation.

Another man sold millions of copies of a book he had written outlining eighty-eight reasons why the Lord would return in 1988. When it didn't happen, he changed it to eighty-nine reasons for 1989, obviously overlooking the many reasons why it could happen in the 1990's, the next century, or even beyond.

Someone else predicted that the world would end on June 9, 1988. He was sure that would be the day! When it didn't happen as predicted, in an attempt to save face, he changed the date to June 9, 1994.

Another person, based on his calculations that a Bible generation was forty-seven and one-third years, predicted that time would end in August of 1991. On the first of September, realizing he must have made a mistake in his calculation, he returned to the drawing board. After carefully checking and rechecking, he postponed the date until 1994. His new date almost coinciding with the June 9, 1994 prophecy of the other person. Yes, I would agree! A mistake was made— and it certainly wasn't made by God!

Those who make and publish these predictions are not near as foolish as those who believe in them and buy such literature. One such book was given to me and, after reading the title, I placed it in its proper place—the trash can! My time is much too important to me to foolishly spend it in hearsay, gossip, debate, and false teaching. In my years of ministry I have read Scripture after Scripture contradicting these false prophets.

> **Matthew 24:36**—But of that day and hour knoweth no *man*, no, not the angels of Heaven, but My Father only.

> **Acts 1:7**—. . . It is not for you to know the times or the seasons, which the Father hath put in His own power.

What dumbfounds me is the multitudes that helped make these men rich. Even after being duped the first time, many of these followers still remain loyal when the false prophet predicts a new date.

Most God-fearing people, including many world leaders, fear the judgment day at the end of time and the ensuing holocaust. *If this were not so, why are so many world leaders and people trying to police the world in an attempt to prevent a nuclear war? Why do nations continually spy on each other to ascertain how much nuclear power and devices they possess.* Daniel 11:24 mentions that devices would be used even unto this day.

JUDGMENT DAY

Hebrews 9:27—And as it is appointed unto men once to die, but after this the judgment . . .

Hebrews 10:26, 27—For if we sin willfully after that we have received the knowledge of the truth, there remaineth no more sacrifice for sins. But a certain fearful looking for of judgment and fiery indignation, which shall devour the adversaries.

Before Christ, the children of Israel, except for those who despised and rejected their way of salvation, were saved by the keeping of the statutes. Esther 8:17 tells us that, ". . . Many of the people of the land became Jews . . ." This meant that people from other nations could join the Judaism faith and be counted as an Israelite. That was then. Now we have Jesus, the Son of the God of Israel, who died on the Cross for the sins of all who believe in Him.

No wonder people fear the end of time, especially those who have not accepted Christ or have trodden the Son of God underfoot. This, of course, includes the Jewish brethren who have heard the truth and rejected His Spirit of Grace.

Hebrews 10:30—. . . The Lord shall judge His people.

Revelation 20:12-15—And I saw the dead small and great, stand before God; and the Books were opened: and another Book was opened, which is *the Book* of Life: and the dead were judged out of those things which were written in the Books, according to their works. And the sea gave up the dead which were in it; and death and Hell delivered up the dead which were in them: and they were judged every man according to their works. And death and Hell were cast into the lake of fire. This is the second death. And whosoever was not found written in the Book of Life was cast into the lake of fire.

This is the judgment of God. God will judge the people of all nations and any not found written in the Book of Life will be cast into the lake of fire. There is no different strokes for different folks—God is no respecter of person or nationality.

Daniel 12:1, 2, 9—And at that time shall Michael stand up, the great prince which standeth for the children of thy people: and there shall be a time of trouble, such as never was since there was a nation *even* to that same time: and at that time thy people shall be delivered, every one that shall be found written in the Book. And many of them that sleep in the dust of the earth shall awake, some to everlasting life, and some

to shame *and* everlasting contempt . . . And
he said, Go thy way, Daniel: for the words
are closed up and sealed till the time of the
end.

"Closed up and sealed till the time of the end." To those
who prophesy and claim that they know when the world will
end and Christ will return, I ask, "Would God give the end
time revelation to false prophets and yet keep the Book closed
up to Daniel?" Not likely!

CHAPTER EIGHTEEN

A WARNING TO THE GENTILES

Romans 11:1-5—I say then, Hath God cast away His people? God forbid. For I also am an Israelite, of the seed of Abraham, of the tribe of Benjamin. God hath not cast away His people which He foreknew. Wot ye not what the Scripture saith of Elias? How he maketh intercession to God against Israel, saying, Lord, they have killed Thy prophets, and digged down Thine altars; and I am left alone, and they seek my life. But what saith the answer of God unto him? I have reserved to myself seven thousand men, who have not bowed the knee to the image of Baal. Even so then at this present time also there is a remnant according to the election of grace.

God has not cast away all His people. He kept a remnant. In 1970 I met a man in Tulsa, Oklahoma who had within him the Spirit of God. This man was a descendent of the tribe of Levi, a Rabbi priest, who had been saved by the election of Grace in Christ Jesus. He said to me, "I count my nationality, my Rabbi linage and inheritance as dung, for I have found my Savior." All can be saved if they choose Jesus, the new covenant!

> **Romans 11:19-22**—Thou wilt say then, The branches were broken off, that I might be graffed in. Well; because of unbelief they were broken off, and thou standest by faith. Be not high-minded, but fear: For if God spared not the natural branches, *take heed* lest He also spare not thee. Behold therefore the goodness and severity of God: on them which fall, severity; but toward thee, goodness, if thou continue in *His* goodness: otherwise thou also shalt be cut off.

God, in First Kings 9:6, 7, promised that He would cut off the Jewish people because of their unbelief. And, He did! *Why?* Because they didn't believe the everlasting promise He made to Abraham. We should learn from their example and take heed that we continue in goodness. *Why?* Because if we sin willfully and fall into His severity, we, the gentiles, shall also be cut off. What happened to the Jews can also happen to the Gentiles.

Some people continue to mistakenly believe that, just because they have been saved by grace, that God would not cut them off. They persist in this false belief and go out to live a life of sin!

> **Romans 11:23**—And they also, if they abide not still in unbelief, shall be graffed in: for God is able to graff them in again.

The people of Israel, as well as those of other nations, desire peace and a land of their own—a place they can call home and raise a family without worry or hunger. A place of utopia! A paradise! A promised land!

The land God promised Abraham could be such a land; however, as long as there are men of greed, envy, and lust in the world, this will not come to pass. When Jesus sets up the Milennial Kingdom, all of the enemies of the soul, and of our tranquility and peace with God and man will be abolished and done away with. Satan and the Beast will not be able keep man from serving God and temptation and sin will no longer enter into the heart and life of man. Jesus said:

> **Matthew 12:39**—. . . *An* evil and adulterous generation seeketh after a sign; and there shall no sign be given to it, but the sign of the prophet Jonas.

Some believe that they can live a long life watching for a sign from God and, as soon as the sign appears, turn to Him. However, Matthew 24:42 plainly teaches that we are to "Watch therefore: for ye know not what hour your Lord doth come." He repeats this in Matthew 25:13, "Watch therefore, for ye know neither the day nor the hour wherein the Son of Man cometh." He does not lie—His Word is truth!

THE SUMMARY

All of God's promises were renewed and passed from generation to generation, with each promise being modified. Each of His promises came with a condition or in the form of a covenant.

After Israel continually broke their covenant with God, He replaced it with a new and better way—He replaced it with Jesus. (Hebrews 10:16 and Jeremiah 31:31)

When God, speaking to His prophet Amos, said, "I will not again pass by them anymore," He was referring to Israel. God, Himself, when He broke the covenant, cancelled and made null and void the promises He had made to worldly Israel.

Jesus said, "My kingdom is not of this world." His Kingdom, the Kingdom of God, is spiritual—a spiritual Israel, a spiritual Jerusalem, and a spiritual church. His people, His chosen people, are His Spiritual church—a church made up of every race, nation, and denomination. It is a Kingdom comprised of only those whose names are written in the Lamb's Book of Life.

The old covenant no longer exists, it is gone, removed by God! If it still existed, then the Blood Jesus shed and His death on the Cross would have no meaning.

Which is it? In Jesus, is it the old or the new covenant?

It can't be both! Before Jesus came there were false prophets and gods and, since His death and resurrection, many false messiahs, cults, and religions have arisen. Some, including those who profess to be Christian, continue to preach everything but Christ; yet, He is the only way. When God said, "This is My beloved Son . . . hear ye Him," He was speaking of Jesus!

Which is it? Does God play favorites? Does He differentiate between Jew and Gentile? If He does, then First Corinthians 12:13, Galatians 3:28, and Colossians 3:13 will have to be removed from the Bible. *Why?* Because they clearly state, "There is neither Greek nor Jew, circumcision nor uncircumcision, bond nor free, but Christ who is all and in all."

First Peter 1:17 states, ". . . who without respect of persons judgeth according to every man's work . . ." God will judge every man according to his work. *Every man* includes Israel for God does not differentiate between persons, or nations. *Should that Scripture also be removed?* If God shows respect to Israel, and Israel alone, we will also have to remove Romans 2:11, Colossians 3:25, and Ephesians 6:9!

The wages of sin is death! All have sinned and come short of the glory of God! It is only by the Blood of Christ that one can be saved!

> **James 2:9**—But if ye have respect to persons, ye commit sin, and are convinced of the law as transgressors.

This Scripture from James was not included in the Bible by accident. *If God shows respect to persons does that mean He is like man?* Heaven forbid! *God a sinner?* Hello! Think about it! In conclusion, the truth of the matter is this:

For God so loved the world,
that He gave His only begotten Son,
that whosoever believeth in Him should
not perish,
but have everlasting life.
(John 3:16)